THE
CHILDREN'S
STEP-BY-STEP
COOK
BOOK

BY
ANGELA WILKES

DK

DORLING KINDERSLEY
LONDON • NEW YORK • STUTTGART

A DORLING KINDERSLEY BOOK

For Sam, Rose, and Roger

Art Editor Jane Bull
Photography Dave King
Home Economist Jane Suthering

Editor Anna Kunst
Managing Art Editor Jacquie Gulliver
Managing Editor Susan Peach

U.S. Editors Jeanette Mall, Chris Benton,
Jill Hamilton, Julee Binder

Production Shelagh Gibson
DTP Designer James W Hunter

Published in the United States by
Dorling Kindersley Inc., 95 Madison Avenue
New York, New York 10016

First American Edition, 1994
2 4 6 8 10 9 7 5 3

Wilkes, Angela.
Children's step-by-step cookbook / by Angela Wilkes.
-- 1st American ed.
p. cm.
Includes index.
ISBN 1-56458-474-7
1. Cookery--Juvenile literature. [1. Cookery.] I. Title.
TX652.5.W548 1994   93-28860
641.5'123--dc20
                                        CIP
                    AC

Reproduced by Bright Arts in Hong Kong
Printed and bound in Italy by New Interlitho, Milan.

CONTENTS

12

SNACKS

CONTENTS

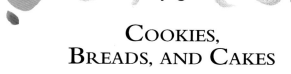

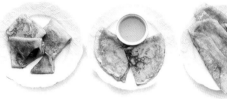

COOKING FOR BEGINNERS

The CHILDREN'S STEP-BY-STEP COOKBOOK is full of easy-to-follow recipes for things that are fun to make and scrumptious to eat. From boiling an egg to creating the perfect apple pie, all the basic cooking skills are covered. You can learn how to make your own bread, whip up meringues, and make delicious sauces, plus there are lots of suggestions on how to vary the recipes. There is also useful information about ingredients and a complete picture glossary.

THE CHAPTER OPENERS

The recipe part of the book is divided into seven chapters, such as "Vegetables." Each chapter starts with simple recipes and progresses to more advanced ones. At the beginning of the chapter there is a double-page information spread on ingredients like this one.

THE PICTURE GLOSSARY

The picture glossary on pages 121-12 explains all the most common cooking terms. Words that appear in the glossary are shown in italic type, like this: *simmer*. Look in the glossary for step-by-step picture guides to particular cooking techniques, such as creaming.

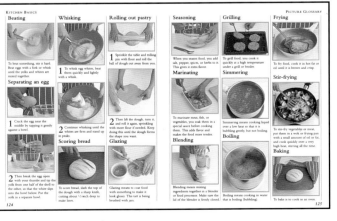

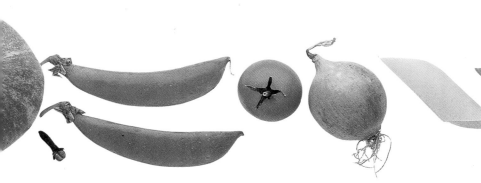

THE RECIPES

The ingredients

All the ingredients you need for each recipe are shown, so that you can check that you have the right amounts.

The quantities

Each recipe tells you how many servings the ingredients make. Generally, each recipe serves four people.

Cook's tools

These illustrated checklists show you all the utensils you need to have ready before you start cooking.

Cook's tools

Quantity

Ingredients

Oven glove symbol

Step-by-step photos

Finished dish

Step-by-step photos

Step-by-step photographs and easy-to-follow instructions show you what to do at each stage of every recipe.

The oven glove symbol

The oven glove symbol means that you have to do something that could be dangerous (such as using the oven, or the blender) and you should ask an adult to help you.

The finishing touches

These pictures show you how to garnish or decorate the things you have made and ways of serving them.

KITCHEN RULES

Cooking is fun, but hot ovens and sharp knives can also make it dangerous, so it is very important to learn some basic safety rules. They are illustrated here to make it easier to remember them. Read the rules carefully and follow them whenever you are cooking.

Be careful!

Never cook anything unless there is an adult there to help you. This oven mitt symbol is a safety warning. Whenever you see the symbol next to a picture, it means you should ask an adult for help. Every time you cut something with a sharp knife, use the oven, or just need advice, ask your adult friend to help you.

Measuring

The recipes give the amount of each ingredient that you will need. All liquid ingredients and many dry ones are measured in units of volume, such as cups or tablespoons, while a few dry ingredients are measured in units of weight, such as ounces. Dry ingredients that are measured by volume should fill the measuring cup or spoon and be level with the top. When the recipe calls for a teaspoon or tablespoon of an ingredient, use special measuring spoons made for cooking. The ingredients measured in ounces can generally be bought in the amount needed for the recipe or in some quantity that is easy to divide into the amount needed.

Using an oven

Always ask an adult to turn on the oven for you. The oven should be switched onto the temperature given in the recipe before you start cooking, so that it will have heated up when you need to use it. Don't open the oven door while things are cooking. Follow the cooking times given in the recipe. And don't forget to turn the oven off when you have finished cooking!

Oven temperatures

Temperatures are shown in Fahrenheit (°F). Water boils at 212°. The temperature settings on most ovens range from 200° to 500°.

1 Before you start cooking, wash your hands and put on an apron. You may need to roll up your sleeves too.

5 When you are cooking on top of the stove, turn the saucepan handles to the side, so you do not knock them.

9 Always wear oven gloves when picking up anything hot, or when putting things into or taking them out of the oven.

2 Collect all the ingredients together. Carefully measure the liquid and dry ingredients in a measuring cup or spoons.

3 Check the recipe as you do this, to make sure that you have everything you need and know exactly what to do.

4 Be very careful with sharp knives. Hold them with the blade pointing downward and always use a cutting board.

6 When you are stirring food in a pan, use a wooden spoon and hold the pan firmly by the handle.

7 Whenever you find it difficult to do something or you have to handle hot things, ask an adult to help you.

8 Have a space ready for hot things. Put them on a mat or a wooden board, not straight onto a table or work surface.

10 Always make sure your hands are dry before you plug in or disconnect an electric appliance, such as a blender.

11 Keep a towel nearby so that you can wipe up any spills. Clean up anything that spills on the floor immediately.

12 Wash up as you go along. When you have finished cooking, put everything away and clean up any mess.

COOK'S TOOLS

Here are all the utensils you will need to follow the recipes in this book. A kitchen scale is useful if you have to weigh anything. You will find a checklist of the cook's tools that you need at the beginning of each recipe.

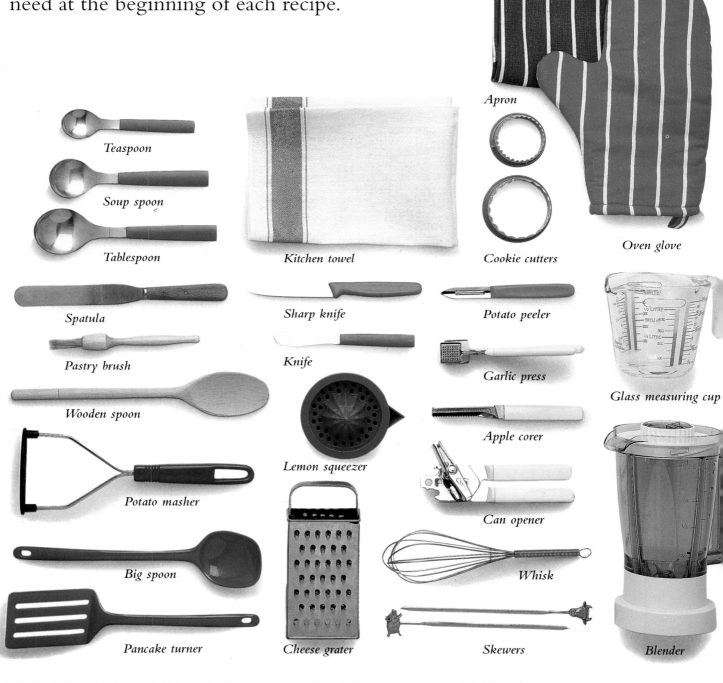

Apron

Teaspoon

Soup spoon

Tablespoon

Kitchen towel

Cookie cutters

Oven glove

Spatula

Sharp knife

Potato peeler

Pastry brush

Knife

Garlic press

Glass measuring cup

Wooden spoon

Lemon squeezer

Apple corer

Potato masher

Can opener

Big spoon

Whisk

Pancake turner

Cheese grater

Skewers

Blender

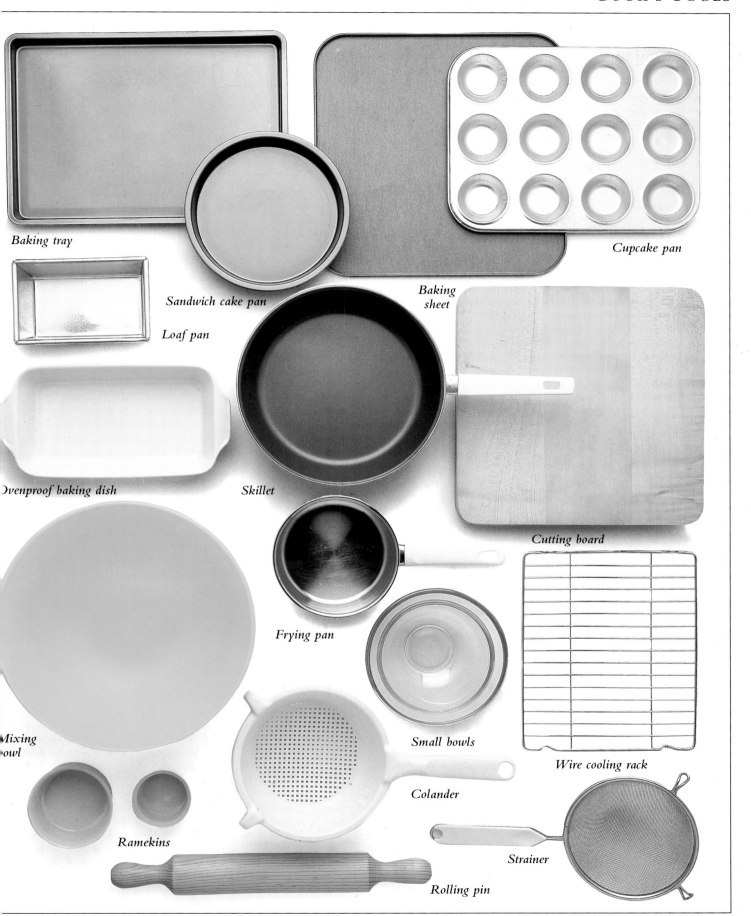

Baking tray

Sandwich cake pan

Loaf pan

Cupcake pan

Baking sheet

Ovenproof baking dish

Skillet

Cutting board

Frying pan

Mixing bowl

Small bowls

Wire cooling rack

Ramekins

Colander

Strainer

Rolling pin

SNACKS

This book starts with snacks because they are quick, easy, and fun to prepare. A snack can be anything that fills those empty moments between main meals. It might be a creamy milk shake, popcorn, or a roll filled with some of your favorite things. Breads and cold meats are features in many snacks. Here you can find out a bit more about them.

BREAD

There are many different types of breads. Try rye bread as well as white and brown bread made from whole-wheat flour. Use sliced bread for sandwiches, stuff flat breads with salad, and look for unusual rolls from different countries.

English muffin　　*Mini-pita bread*

Whole-wheat mini-pita bread

Sliced white bread　　*Pumpernickel bread*　　*Sliced whole-wheat bread*

Italian white roll

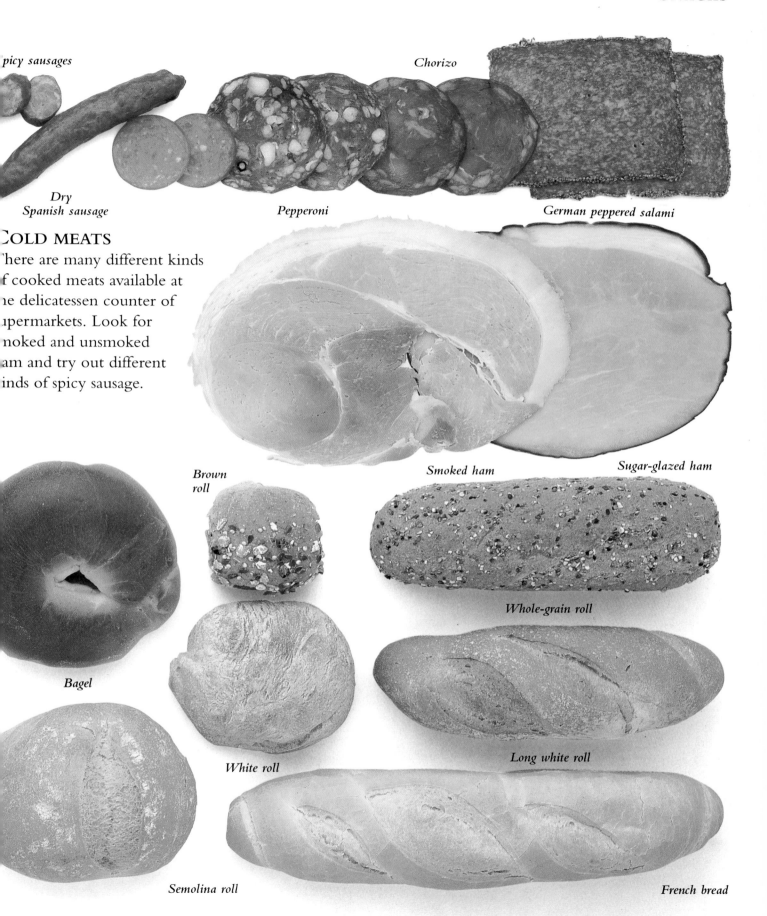

picy sausages

Chorizo

*Dry
Spanish sausage*

Pepperoni

German peppered salami

COLD MEATS

There are many different kinds of cooked meats available at the delicatessen counter of supermarkets. Look for smoked and unsmoked ham and try out different kinds of spicy sausage.

Smoked ham

Sugar-glazed ham

*Brown
roll*

Whole-grain roll

Bagel

White roll

Long white roll

Semolina roll

French bread

SNACKS ON STICKS

You can make simple kabobs with whatever you have at home. Try creating fruity ones, cheesy ones, or mixing sweet things with salty things. Choose contrasting colors and mix soft things with crunchy things. Here are some to try.

You will need

(for 5 kabobs)

Baby corn

A green pepper

A carrot

Canned mandarin oranges

Small tomatoes

Strawberries

A small bunch of grapes

A hard cheese

Salami

Pineapple cubes

Mozzarella cheese

Button mushrooms

A peach

Small cooked beets

Snow peas

Sliced ham

Stuffed olives

Cooked hot dogs

COOK'S TOOLS

Sharp knife • Potato peeler
Cutting board • Wooden skewers

What to do

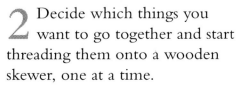

1 Cut the cheese and hot dogs into chunks. Cut cubes of green pepper. Cut the carrot in half and peel it into long strips.

2 Decide which things you want to go together and start threading them onto a wooden skewer, one at a time.

3 Continue threading things onto the skewer until it is full, with just enough room at each end to hold it.

Rainbow kabobs

The finished kabobs are a good picnic or party treat. Slide everything off the skewer onto a plate with a fork. If not eaten at once, store in the refrigerator.

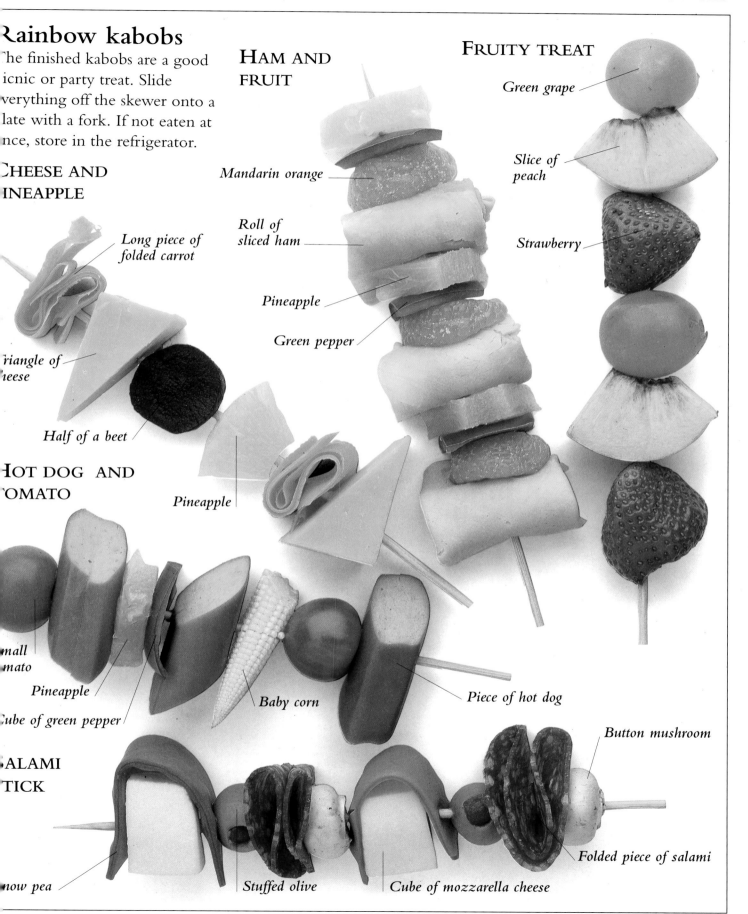

CHEESE AND PINEAPPLE

Long piece of folded carrot

Triangle of cheese

Half of a beet

Pineapple

HOT DOG AND TOMATO

Small tomato

Pineapple

Cube of green pepper

SALAMI STICK

Snow pea

Baby corn

Piece of hot dog

Stuffed olive

Cube of mozzarella cheese

Button mushroom

Folded piece of salami

HAM AND FRUIT

Mandarin orange

Roll of sliced ham

Pineapple

Green pepper

FRUITY TREAT

Green grape

Slice of peach

Strawberry

SANDWICH FILLINGS

Sandwiches and filled rolls are perfect snack food. On the next four pages you will find some ideas on how to use fillings in a variety of rolls and open sandwiches. It is best to store them in the refrigerator and eat within 24 hours.

You will need (for 6 servings)

For avocado filling

1 avocado   *1 finely chopped tomato*   *2 tablespoons crème fraiche or sour cream*

For any of the fillings

A pinch of salt

A pinch of pepper

For tuna filling

1 small can of tuna   *2 tablespoons mayonnaise*   *1 finely chopped celery rib*   *1 finely chopped scallion*

For ham and chicken filling

3 tablespoons crème fraiche   *1/3 cup diced ham*   *1 diced cooked skinned chicken breast*   *1 tablespoon chopped parsley*

For egg filling

1 tablespoon sprouts

For creamy cheese filling

1/4 diced red pepper

For carrot and cheese filling

1 cup grated carrot   *1 tablespoon salad dressing (see page 56)*   *1 cup grated cheese*   *1 peeled grated apple*

1 tablespoon mayonnaise   *2 hard-boiled eggs*   *4 oz cream cheese*   *2 tablespoons chopped cucumber*

CARROT AND CHEESE

TUNA

CREAM CHEESE

Carrot and cheese

Put the *grated* cheese, carrot, and apple in a bowl. Add the salad dressing, salt, and pepper and mix everything together.

Tuna

Put the finely *chopped* scallion and celery in a bowl with the drained tuna, mayonnaise, salt, and pepper and stir well.

Creamy cheese

Beat the cream cheese in a bowl with a fork until smooth, then mix in the red pepper, cucumber, salt, and pepper.

Ham and chicken

Beat the crème fraiche in a bowl until it is smooth, then stir in the ham, chicken, parsley, salt, and pepper.

Egg salad

Boil the eggs in the saucepan (see page 28), then mash them in a bowl. Add the sprouts, mayonnaise, salt, and pepper.

Avocado

Cut the avocado in half, then remove the pit and skin. Mash the flesh in a bowl, then stir in the tomato and crème fraiche.

HAM AND CHICKEN

EGG SALAD

AVOCADO

FINGER BITES

When you want something special for a snack or a party, have fun creating these tiny sandwiches, where everything is arranged on top of firm bread or toast. Try the ideas shown here, or invent some of your own. Eat immediately.

You will need

Sliced firm bread, such as pumpernickel   *Stuffed olives*   *Cherry tomatoes*

Long whole-grain rolls

Round rolls or English muffins

Tuna filling (see page 16)

Shredded lettuce

Cream cheese

Creamy scrambled egg (see page 30)

Sliced ham and cheese

Currants or raisins   *Canned red kidney beans*

Strips of pepper

Sliced carrots

Sliced radishes

Sliced cucumber

Sprouts

COOK'S TOOLS

Cookie cutters • Teaspoon • Knife
Sharp knife • Cutting board

Funny faces

1 Cut an English muffin or a bread roll in half. You can use each half to make a funny face sandwich.

2 Cut out a circle of sliced cheese and lay it on the roll. Add a mouth cut out of cheese and two slices of cucumber.

3 Use lettuce for eyebrows and two halves of tomato for eyes. Stick a kidney bean to the face with cream cheese for a nose.

Tutti-frutti ice cream

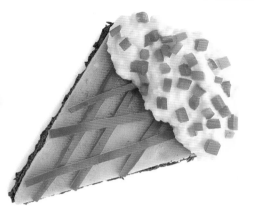

1 Take a slice of bread and cut the ends off diagonally so that it takes the shape of an ice cream cone, as shown above.

2 Cut out a triangle of ham for the cone and lay it on the bread. Spoon scrambled egg above it to look like ice cream.

3 Lay strips of red pepper in a crisscross pattern on the cone and sprinkle finely *diced* peppers on the scrambled egg.

Woolly sheep

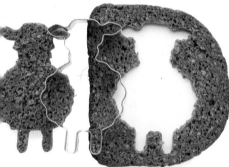

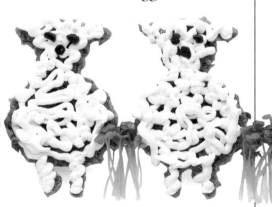

1 Use a cookie cutter to cut sheep out of slices of brown bread. Or use the cutters you have to cut out other animals.

2 Spread cream cheese over the sheep. If the cheese is in a tube, squeeze it out in wiggly lines to look like wool.

3 Add currants to make eyes and noses and snip off tiny bunches of sprouts to make green grass for munching.

Freddy flounder

1 Take a long roll and slice off one end. Then cut out two triangles – one at the top and one at the bottom of the roll.

2 Spread tuna filling over the roll. Then arrange slices of cucumber and radish on top to overlap like scales.

3 Add triangles of sliced carrot for fins and half an olive for an eye, and make a mouth out of squares of red pepper.

MEALS IN ROLLS

Filled rolls don't just make good snacks. You can eat them as snacks or at picnics and parties. Try using different sorts of bread and mixing the fillings you have made with crunchy salad vegetables and ham, cheese, or sausage. Eat within 24 hours.

You will need (for 5 rolls)

Different kinds of rolls

White roll

Italian round roll

Small pita breads

Whole-grain roll or torpedo with seeds on top

Sliced salami

Small lettuce leaves

Strips of bacon or smoked ham

Tomatoes

Sliced cheese

Sliced ham

Mayonnaise

Butter

Tuna filling (see pages 16–17)

Egg salad (see pages 16–17)

Avocado filling (see pages 16–17)

Greek salad (see pages 56–57)

What to do

1 Carefully cut along each roll lengthwise, then open the roll and spread both halves with a little butter or mayonnaise.

2 Spoon filling onto one half of the roll (or into the bread if using pita bread). Spread the filling with a knife.

3 Arrange the other ingredient on top. These slices of salam are folded in half, then in half again to make a butterfly shape.

MINI-PITAS

Greek salad

Whole-wheat
pita bread

ROUND ROLL

Tuna filling

Sliced tomato

Lettuce

Round roll

Avocado filling

Cooked bacon
or smoked ham

White pita bread

TORPEDO

WHITE ROLL

Lettuce

Sliced cheese

Sliced tomato

Egg salad

Sliced ham

Folded salami

FROZEN FRUIT BARS

What better snack on a hot day than a frozen fruit bar? Here you can find out how to make your own from fruit juice and fruit yogurt. The quantities shown will make about three of each flavor. They will take about two hours to freeze.

COOK'S TOOLS

*Frozen bar molds and sticks
Cutting board • Sharp knife • Spoon
Bowl • Glass measuring cup*

You will need (for 6 bars)

For fruity yogurt bar

5 tablespoons raspberry syrup

2/3 cup strawberry yogurt

For orange fruit bar

*1/2 cup
mixed orange juice and apricot nectar*

*2/3 cup chopped
mixed canned fruit*

FROZEN FRUIT BARS

Fruity Yogurt bar

Mix the yogurt and raspberry syrup together, then pour the mixture into the molds and put them in the freezer.

Orange Fruit bar

Drain the fruit and put it in a bowl. Mix in the fruit juice, then pour the mixture into the molds and put in the freezer.

To remove the bars from the molds, hold them upside down under warm running water for a few seconds and ease them out.

POPCORN

Making popcorn is like a magic trick, and it tastes good! You can buy many kinds of popping corn at supermarkets. Serve it warm with melted butter and add salt or sugar, depending on how you like it. Be extra careful when you make popcorn this way.

You will need (for 4 servings)

2 tablespoons vegetable oil

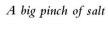

A big pinch of salt

1 tablespoon butter

1/3 cup popping corn

2 tablespoons brown sugar (if you like)

POPCORN

Why not use a pastry bag as a cone?

What to do

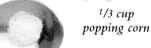

1 Heat the vegetable oil in the saucepan until hot. Then add enough corn to cover the bottom of the pan in a single layer.

2 Cook the corn until it starts to pop, then put the lid on the pan. Shake the pan over medium heat until all the corn has popped.

3 Take the lid off the pan, add butter and salt or sugar, and stir the popcorn. Then eat it at once.

MILK SHAKES

Here is a recipe for a scrumptious banana milk shake. You can also make it in other flavors – just leave out the banana and use the alternatives shown below to make a raspberry or chocolate shake. There is enough for one large milk shake.

You will need (for 1 large shake)

1 tablespoon vanilla ice cream

1 tablespoon honey

For banana milk shake

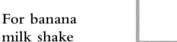

1 banana

For chocolate milk shake

6 chocolate sandwich cookies

²/₃ cup milk

¹/₃ cup plain yogurt

For raspberry milk shake

³/₄ cup raspberries

What to do

1 Peel and slice the banana. If you are making a chocolate milk shake, break the cookies into large pieces.

2 Put all the ingredients for the milk shake into the *blender*, put the lid on, and whiz it for about one minute.

3 Take the top off the blender. The milk shake should be evenly mixed and creamy. Pour it into a tall glass immediately.

Snack in a drink

Serve the milk shakes with straws.
If you like, you can decorate the
shakes with sliced bananas, grated
chocolate, or raspberries.

CHOCOLATE
SHAKE

RASPBERRY DREAM

BANANA SHAKE

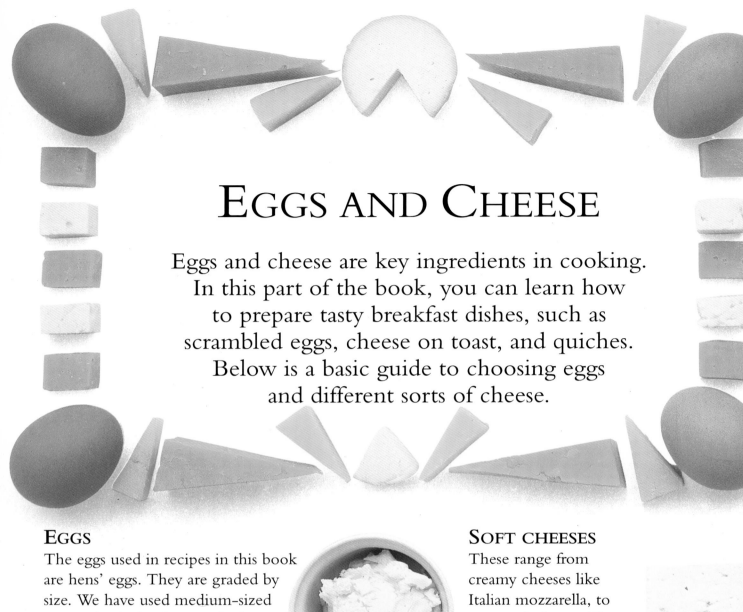

EGGS AND CHEESE

Eggs and cheese are key ingredients in cooking.
In this part of the book, you can learn how
to prepare tasty breakfast dishes, such as
scrambled eggs, cheese on toast, and quiches.
Below is a basic guide to choosing eggs
and different sorts of cheese.

EGGS

The eggs used in recipes in this book
are hens' eggs. They are graded by
size. We have used medium-sized
eggs. Check the date on the box
to make sure the eggs are fresh.

Cream cheese

Eggs

Sour cream

SOFT CHEESES

These range from
creamy cheeses like
Italian mozzarella, to
semi-soft cheeses like
Greek feta.

Feta cheese

Mozzarella

HARD CHEESES

These cheeses are firm, with a strong taste, and are the ones most often used for flavoring in cooking. They are usually *grated* before being added to other ingredients. When sliced, they are delicious eaten with crusty bread or crackers.

Parmesan

Grated Parmesan

White Cheddar

Cheddar

Gruyère

Sliced white Cheddar

Sliced Cheddar

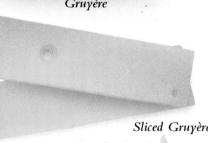

Sliced Gruyère

Grated white Cheddar

Grated Cheddar

Grated Gruyère

SPECIAL CHEESES

Cheeses like these are usually eaten with bread or crackers. Each of them has a special flavor of its own. Choose two or three contrasting cheeses to serve on a cheeseboard.

Crottin (small goat's cheese)

Stilton (blue cheese)

Brie

As with all cheeses, buy these cut fresh rather than packaged in plastic.

BOILED EGGS

Boiled eggs are about the easiest thing to cook and make a delicious breakfast or quick meal. Eat them hot with a little salt and pepper and buttered bread or toast. Hard-boiled eggs are useful for picnics or for adding to salads.

COOK'S TOOLS

Big spoon • Saucepan Small bowl

You will need (for 3 servings)

SOFT-BOILED EGGS

3 eggs

The whites are firm but the yolks are still soft

HARD–BOILED EGGS

Both the yolks and whites are firm

What to do

1 Heat some water in a saucepan until it is *simmering*. Then lower the eggs into the water on a big spoon.

2 Boil the eggs for 6 to 7 minutes, then lift them out of the pan. To hard-boil eggs, cook them for 10 to 12 minutes.

3 Put hard-boiled eggs in a bowl of cold water. Tap each one against the bowl to crack its shell, then peel off the shells.

EGGS IN POTS

Baked eggs are easy to make and can be a breakfast or a quick meal. To vary them, you can tuck some cheese, ham, or cooked vegetables under the egg as a surprise. It is best to bake eggs in the small straight-sided dishes called ramekins (see page 11).

(see page 11)

COOK'S TOOLS

Baking sheet • Teaspoon
Cheese grater • Ramekins

You will need (for 3 servings)

1/4 cup grated cheese

1 egg per person

3 tablespoons light cream

Pepper

Salt

For variations

1/4 cup cooked spinach

or 2 tablespoons tomato sauce

or 1 slice of garlic sausage or ham

SPINACH SURPRISE

HAM SURPRISE

TOMATO SURPRISE

What to do

1 Set the oven to 375°F. Butter the ramekins and put in the cooked spinach, tomato sauce, or ham.

2 Add salt and pepper if you like, then break an egg into each ramekin. Spoon the cream on top and add the *grated* cheese.

3 Set the ramekins on the baking sheet and bake them for 15 to 25 minutes, until the whites of the eggs are firm.

SCRAMBLED EGGS

This is one of the simplest yet most delicious ways of cooking eggs. The secret to making good scrambled eggs is to cook them over very low heat and keep stirring them. They should take about five minutes to cook.

You will need (for 1 serving)

For basic scrambled egg

A pat of butter

2 tablespoons milk

2 eggs

A pinch of pepper

A pinch of salt

For ham scramble

1/3 cup diced ham

Small sprig of parsley

For Spanish scramble

1 tablespoon vegetable oil

1/4 cup sliced pepperoni

1/4 red pepper and 1/4 green pepper

Basic scrambled eggs

1 Break the eggs into the bowl. Add the milk, salt, and pepper and *beat* everything together until well mixed.

2 Melt the butter in the saucepan over low heat until foaming. Swirl it around the pan, then pour in the eggs.

3 Cook the eggs over low heat, stirring them as they begin to thicken. They are ready when creamy and nearly set.

Spanish scramble

1 *Slice* the peppers finely. Then heat the oil in the saucepan and cook the peppers in it for a few minutes.

2 Add the peppers and pepperoni to the basic egg mixture. Cook the eggs as before in a saucepan with melted butter.

Ham scramble

Cut the ham into cubes and *chop* the parsley. Add the ham and parsley to the basic egg mixture and cook the eggs as before.

Creamy eggs

Serve the eggs immediately while hot. Garnish them with toast or fried bread cut into shapes with cookie cutters.

SPANISH SCRAMBLE

HAM SCRAMBLE

Diamond-shaped pieces of toast

Chicken made of toast

PLAIN SCRAMBLED EGGS

FRENCH TOAST AND CINNAMON TOAST

Here you can find out how to make French toast (sometimes called eggy bread) and cinnamon toast, which is a sweet version of it. Neither is really toast, but fried bread. It makes a wonderful breakfast treat.

COOK'S TOOLS

Bowl • Frying pan • Cookie cutter
Pancake turner • Fork

You will need

(for 2-3 servings)

One egg for each type of toast

For frying

2 tablespoons
butter

1 tablespoon vegetable oil

3 slices of bread for each egg

For French toast

Large pinches of salt and pepper (optional)

For cinnamon toast

1 teaspoon
ground cinnamon

2 tablespoons
sugar

French toast

1 Break an egg into the bowl. Add the salt and pepper and *beat* the egg with a fork until it is evenly mixed and frothy.

2 Dip each slice of bread into the beaten egg, so that the bread is evenly coated with egg on both sides.

3 Heat the butter and oil in the frying pan. When the pan is hot, fry the bread on both sides until it is golden brown.

Cinnamon toast

1 Cut stars out of the sliced bread with the cookie cutter. Press the cutter down on the bread, then lift out the stars.

2 Break the egg into the bowl and add the ground cinnamon and half of the sugar. *Beat* the egg with a fork and dip the stars in it.

3 Heat the butter and oil in the frying pan and fry the stars for about 2 to 3 minutes on each side until they are crisp and brown.

FRENCH TOAST

Cut the French toast into chunky triangles

Serve apple butter, jam, or maple syrup for dipping

Sprinkle the remaining sugar onto the cinnamon stars once they have cooled a little

CINNAMON TOAST

TOASTY TREATS

Grilled cheese on toast is a tasty quick snack or an easy meal. Why not have fun and turn it into something special by using different sorts of bread and cheese and by inventing different toppings? Here are some ideas to try.

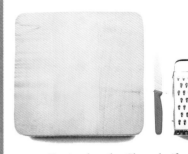
You will need
(for 1 serving of each toast)

For apple toast

A slice of French bread

1 tablespoon grated cheese　*¼ red apple*

A pat of butter

For tic-tac-toe

A slice of brown bread

Narrow strips of ham

A slice of cheese

A pitted black olive

Strips of contrasting cheese

For the flower pizza

½ teaspoon finely chopped red onion

Half a round roll

2 small tomatoes

2 tablespoons grated mozzarella

2 tiny mushrooms

1 teaspoon grated cheese

What to do

1 Carefully slice the apple, tomatoes, and mushrooms. Cut the olive into O's. Cut the ham into small strips.

2 Follow the pictures on the opposite page to see how to arrange the different ingredients on each piece of bread.

3 Heat the broiler until hot, then put the pieces of bread on the grill pan and *grill* them until cheese on top is bubbling.

Apple toast

1 Butter the piece of toasted French bread lightly. Cover it with overlapping slices of apple.

2 Sprinkle a layer of grated cheese over the slices of apple, making sure the bread is evenly covered in the middle.

3 Put the piece of bread under the grill and cook it until the cheese has melted and is bubbling nicely.

Tic-tac-toe

1 Turn on the grill and grill the piece of brown bread until it lightly toasted on one side.

2 Lay a slice of cheese on the untoasted side of the bread. Decorate with the strips of cheese, ham, and sliced olive.

3 Heat the grill and place the toast under it. The toast will be ready when the cheese has melted and is bubbling gently.

Flower pizza

1 Sprinkle the mozzarella cheese on the cut side of the roll. Grill until cheese melts. Arrange sliced tomatoes on top.

2 Lay sliced mushrooms on the tomatoes and put the chopped onion in the middle of them. Sprinkle with grated cheese.

3 Put the roll under the heated grill and toast it until the grated cheese has melted and is bubbling.

QUICHES AND TARTS

Making pastry is easy once you know how! Here you can find out how to make a classic Quiche Lorraine or four tiny tarts using the same pastry and basic filling. You will need only half the basic filling for the tiny tarts.

You will need (for 4 servings)

For basic filling

For pastry

1 cup all–purpose flour

A pinch of salt

2–3 tablespoons water

2 tablespoons butter

2 tablespoons lard or
vegetable shortening

1 1/3 cups
light cream

Salt
and
pepper

2 eggs

For Quiche Lorraine

3/4 cup grated
Gruyère cheese

4 slices of bacon

What to do

1 Set the oven to 400°F. Cut up the butter and lard and put them in the bowl with the flour and a pinch of salt.

2 *Rub* the butter, flour, and lard together with your fingertips until they look like fine bread crumbs.

3 Mix in the water a little at a time until you have a soft ball of *dough* that leaves the sides of the bowl clean.

For spinach tarts

*¹/₂ cup grated
Cheddar cheese*

*²/₃ cup thawed frozen
or cooked spinach*

4 slices of tomato

2 scallions

For asparagus tarts

*12 cooked, thawed, or
canned asparagus tips*

*¹/₂ cup grated
Gruyère cheese*

For zucchini and mushroom tarts

*¹/₂ tablespoon
butter for
frying*

4 mushrooms

*¹/₂ cup grated
Cheddar cheese*

For tomato and Parmesan tarts

4 tomatoes

¹/₂ cup grated Parmesan cheese

1 small zucchini

4 Sprinkle flour on the table and on the rolling pin. *Roll* the ball of dough out into a circle until it is quite thin.

5 Check that the pastry is big enough, then lay it in the quiche pan. Press it gently into place and trim the edges.

6 For the tarts, break the dough into four pieces. Roll each piece into a ball, then press it down and roll it out into a circle.

Baking the pastry

7 Lay each circle of pastry over a tart pan and press it into place. Roll the rolling pin over it to trim the edges of pastry.

8 Line each pastry case with a piece of aluminum foil and fill it with dried beans. *Bake* the pastry cases for 15 minutes.

9 Take the pastry cases out of the oven. Let them cool for a minute, then carefully lift out the aluminum foil and beans.

Filling the quiche

1 Chop the bacon into small cubes and fry it quickly in the skillet until crisp. Spread the bacon across the pastry.

2 Break the eggs into a measuring cup. Add the cream, salt, and pepper and *beat* together with a fork. *Grate* the cheese.

3 Pour the egg mixture over the bacon and sprinkle the cheese on top. Bake it for about 25 minutes, until firm.

Filling the tarts

1 Slice the mushrooms and tomatoes. Cut the zucchini into short sticks (you need 3/4 cup) and chop the scallions finely.

2 Arrange the fillings inside the pastry. Mix one egg, 2/3 cup cream, salt, and pepper together in a measuring cup.

3 Pour the egg mixture into the tart cases and sprinkle cheese on top. Bake the tarts for about 1 minutes, until firm and set.

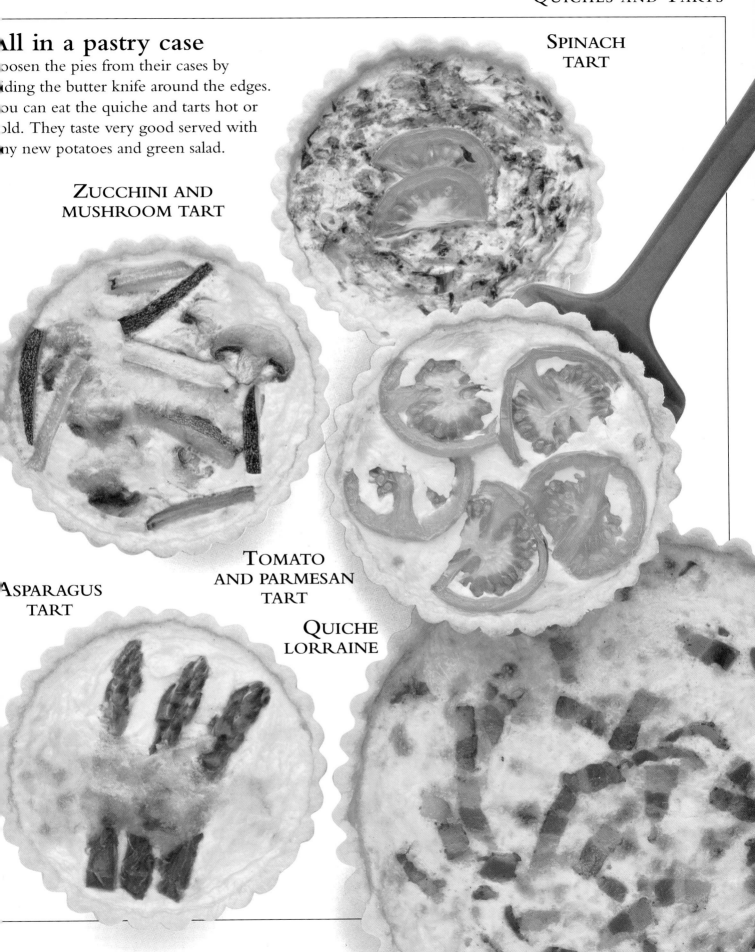

All in a pastry case

oosen the pies from their cases by
iding the butter knife around the edges.
ou can eat the quiche and tarts hot or
old. They taste very good served with
ny new potatoes and green salad.

SPINACH
TART

ZUCCHINI AND
MUSHROOM TART

TOMATO
AND PARMESAN
TART

ASPARAGUS
TART

QUICHE
LORRAINE

PASTA, RICE, AND PIZZA

In this part of the book you can learn how to make some delicious, filling meals, all based on pasta, rice, and pizza. There are many different kinds of rice and pasta, and an endless variety of simple, tasty ways to prepare them. Listed below are some of the many types available.

RICE

Long-grain rice is used for savory dishes and short-grain rice for risottos and puddings. Whole-grain rice is brown. White rice has had the outer husks of the grain removed. It is less healthy than brown rice but it cooks more quickly.

White long-grain rice

Basmati rice

Arborio rice

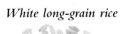

Brown long-grain rice

White short-grain rice

PASTA

Pasta comes either fresh or dried. Dried pasta takes about 10 to 20 minutes to cook and fresh pasta cooks in about three minutes. Plain pasta made with all-purpose flour is yellow. Whole-wheat pasta is brown. Green pasta has spinach added to it, red pasta tomato paste, and pink pasta beet juice.

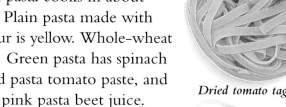
Dried tomato tagliatelle

FLAT PASTA

Pasta also comes in all shapes and sizes, each shape with its own Italian name. Spaghetti and tagliatelle are two types of long, thin pasta. Lasagne are wide ribbons of pasta used for baked dishes of layered pasta – called lasagne!

Fresh green tagliatelle

Dried green tagliatelle

Fresh tagliatelle

Green lasagne

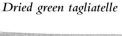
Whole-wheat spaghetti

Plain spaghetti

Green spaghetti

White lasagne

Whole-wheat lasagne

TUBE PASTA

You can buy dried pasta in many different-shaped tubes, ranging from small macaroni to large, ribbed rigatoni or penne. These types of pasta are good served with rich, chunky, meaty sauces.

Rigatoni

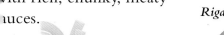
Macaroni

Quills (penne)

INTERESTING SHAPES

Pasta bows, shells, and twists fall into this group, along with lots of other unusual shapes. The smaller shapes are sometimes used in soups. The larger ones can be served with any sauce.

Shells (conchiglie)

Bows (farfalle)

Twists (fusilli)

CREAMY SPAGHETTI

Here you can learn how to cook pasta (spaghetti in this case) and see how to turn it into a delicious quick meal by adding a few ingredients. This recipe is for a carbonara sauce. Turn the page to find out how to make tomato and meat sauces for pasta.

Turn the page to find out how to make tomato and meat sauces for pasta.

COOK'S TOOLS

*Skillet • Wooden spoon
Cutting board • Fork
Cheese grater • Large saucepan
Small bowl • Colander*

You will need (for 4 servings)

³/4 lb spaghetti or other long pasta

3 eggs

Freshly ground black pepper

Salt

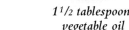

*1¹/2 tablespoons
vegetable oil*

*¹/2 cup
finely grated
Parmesan cheese*

*2 tablespoons
heavy cream*

*4 slices of bacon,
chopped*

What to do

1 Heat some water in a big saucepan. Add a teaspoon of salt and a drop of oil to stop the pasta from sticking together.

2 When the water boils, gently push the pasta into the water until covered. Long pasta slides down as the ends soften.

3 While the pasta cooks, *beat* the eggs in a bowl. Add the cream, salt, pepper, and half the cheese and whisk again.

4 Put the oil in the skillet. Add the chopped bacon and fry it quickly for a few minutes until it is cooked.

5 Cook the pasta for 12 to 15 minutes, until it is cooked but still firm. Then pour it into a colander and drain it well.

6 Put the pasta back into the saucepan. Add the egg mixture and bacon. Stir well and cook it for a few more minutes.

Creamy pasta

Put the spaghetti carbonara in a serving dish and sprinkle the rest of the grated Parmesan cheese on top. Then eat it immediately while it is piping hot.

Grated Parmesan cheese

Pieces of bacon

PASTA SAUCES

Here are two classic pasta sauces – a tomato sauce and a meat (or Bolognese) sauce – which you can make from the same basic recipe. Serve them with ¾ lb pasta for four people. Make the sauce first and cook the pasta last, when you are ready to eat.

COOK'S TOOLS

Saucepan • Cutting board
Can opener • Garlic press • Wooden spoon
Sharp knife • Potato peeler

You will need (for 4 servings)

1 celery rib

1 small carrot

1 clove garlic

½ teaspoon salt

½ teaspoon pepper

1 14-oz can of tomatoes

3 tablespoons tomato puree

2 tablespoons olive oil

1 small onion

For tomato sauce

⅔ cup water

For Bolognese sauce

3 slices of bacon

¾ lb ground beef

Tomato sauce

1 *Chop* the onion, carrot, and celery finely. *Peel* and *crush* the garlic. Heat the oil in the pan, then add the vegetables.

2 Cook the vegetables gently for about 5 minutes, until soft. Add the tomatoes, tomato puree, and water and stir.

3 Let the sauce *simmer* for about 45 minutes, stirring it from time to time. Taste it and add salt and pepper if needed.

Meat (or Bolognese) sauce

1 Chop the vegetables and bacon. Heat the oil in the pan and cook the vegetables for about 5 minutes.

2 Add the ground beef and chopped bacon. Stir them and cook until the meat has browned, stirring all the time.

3 Stir in the canned tomatoes and tomato puree. Heat the sauce, then let it simmer gently for 45 minutes.

PASTA WITH MEAT SAUCE

Meat sauce goes best with long pasta like spaghetti or tagliatelle. Sprinkle it with grated Parmesan cheese for extra flavor.

PASTA WITH TOMATO SAUCE

Mix the tomato sauce into the pasta. Here it is served with squiggly pasta known as orecchiette ("little ears" in Italian). Delicately flavored tomato sauce is good with small, chunky pasta.

VEGETABLES AND RICE

Learn the basic method for cooking rice and see how to use it as the base for a wonderful meal. Prepare the vegetables while the rice is cooking, then keep the rice warm while you quickly fry the vegetables over high heat – it's delicious!

You will need

(for 4 servings)

¼ small head of Chinese cabbage

8-10 mushrooms

2 zucchini

1 small onion

1 tablespoon butter

1 clove garlic

1 small head of broccoli

1-2 tablespoons soy sauce

2 cups water

2 carrots

2 tablespoons vegetable oil

1 cup long-grain rice

1 teaspoon salt

Cooking the rice

1 Melt the butter in a big saucepan over low heat. Add the rice, stir well, and cook for a few minutes, until transparent.

2 Add the water and salt; bring to a boil. Stir once, put a lid on the pan, and cook the rice for 15 to 20 minutes.

3 The rice is cooked when it is tender and has absorbed all the water. Bite a few grains to check whether it is done.

Preparing the vegetables

4 Cut the zucchini and carrots into sticks. *Slice* the onion, mushrooms, and Chinese cabbage, and cut up the broccoli.

5 Heat the oil in the frying pan. Add the onion, crushed garlic, carrots, and broccoli, and stir over a high heat for 5 minutes or so.

6 Add the other vegetables and stir them over a high heat until just tender. Pour the soy sauce into the pan and stir well.

Vegetables on a bed of rice

Turn the rice out onto a serving dish. Spread it out, then arrange the stir-fried vegetables on top and serve the meal at once, while hot.

CHINESE FRIED RICE

This wonderful fried rice is a meal in itself and takes only about 10 minutes to cook once everything is prepared. You can vary the recipe by adding other things you like – perhaps diced cooked chicken or sliced mushrooms.

You will need (for 4 servings)

For boiling the rice

The remaining ingredients

1 tablespoon butter

1 3/4 cups water

1 teaspoon salt

1 1/4 cups long-grain rice

2 eggs

1/2 teaspoon salt

1 cup peas

A cube of fresh ginger root about 1 inch square

1 clove garlic

1/2 small head of Chinese cabbage

1/2 lb peeled small shrimp

2/3 cup water or chicken stock

1 tablespoon s[...] sau[...]

1 small onion

1 tablespoon vegetabl[...]

What to do

1 Cook the rice as shown on page 46. Cook the peas in boiling, slightly salted water for 5 minutes, then drain them.

2 *Peel* the ginger and chop it finely. Peel and *crush* the garlic. *Slice* the onion and the Chinese cabbage.

3 Heat the oil in a large skillet and *fry* the onion, garlic, and ginger in it gently, stirring constantly for about 5 minutes.

4 Add the sliced Chinese cabbage to the skillet. Cook it over high heat for about a minute, stirring all the time.

5 Add the rice, water, and soy sauce, then the shrimp and peas. Stir everything together and cook it for a few minutes.

6 *Beat* the eggs. Make a hollow in the rice, pour in the eggs, and cook them for a few minutes, then stir them into the rice.

A taste of the East

Since this is a meal full of interesting flavors, why not take the Asian theme a bit further? You could serve the rice in bowls and maybe even try using chopsticks!

Shrimp

Peas

Sliced Chinese cabbage

PIZZA FEAST

You can make scrumptious pizzas using this quick recipe. There are three different toppings to try, or you can experiment with ideas of your own. The quantities given will make four mini-pizzas or one big one.

COOK'S TOOLS

Baking sheet • Mixing bowl
Skillet • Rolling pin
Cutting board • Sharp knife
Cheese grater • Wooden spoon

You will need
(for 4 servings)

2 cups self-rising flour

4 tablespoons butter

7–8 tablespoons milk

¹/₂ teaspoon salt

For the tomato sauce

1 small can of tomatoes

Salt and pepper

1 teaspoon sugar

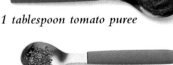

1 tablespoon tomato puree

A pinch of oregano or Italian seasoning

For the toppings

Pitted black olives

Capers

Grated Cheddar cheese

Sliced mushrooms

¹/₂ tomato

Sliced zucchini

Finely sliced onions

Finely grated mozzarella cheese

Sliced spicy sausage

Sliced pepperoni

Chopped ham

Canned tuna

Tomato sauce

Cook all the ingredients for the tomato sauce together in the skillet for about 10 minutes to thicken them.

Making the pizza

1 Set the oven to 425°F. *Rub* the flour, salt, and butter together in a mixing bowl with your fingertips.

2 When the mixture looks like bread crumbs, add the milk and stir everything together into a smooth ball of *dough*.

3 Cut the dough in four and roll each piece into a ball. Roll these out into circles about inches across.

4 Lay the circles of dough on the greased baking sheet. Spread tomato sauce over them to just within the edges.

5 Add toppings to the pizzas, then *bake* them in the oven for 15 to 20 minutes, until the crusts are golden brown.

All on a pizza

Choose two or three things that taste good together for the top of each pizza and arrange them as attractively as you can.

TUNA PIZZA

Black olive

Caper

Canned tuna

Grated mozzarella cheese

Sliced onion

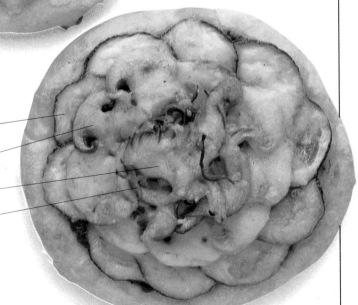

HAM AND PEPPERONI PIZZA

Chopped ham

Grated mozzarella cheese

Sliced pepperoni

ZUCCHINI PIZZA

Sliced zucchini

Sliced mushroom

Grated cheese

Sliced onion

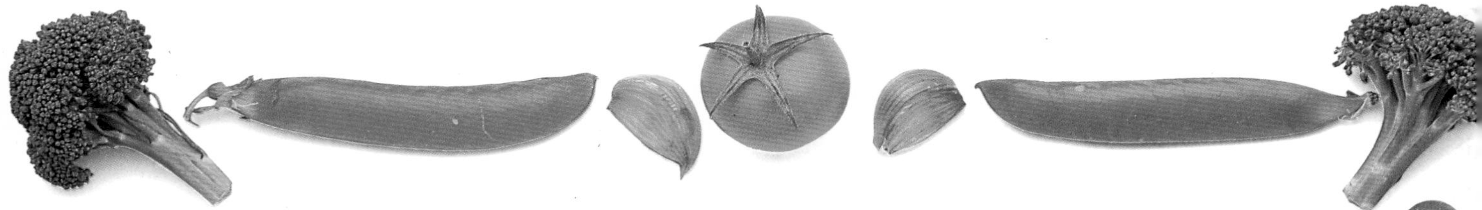

VEGETABLES

In this part of the book you will learn
how to bring out the best in vegetables
by cooking them properly. There are many kinds
of vegetables available to chose from. You will
discover how to create colorful salads and turn
the humble potato into a feast fit for a king.
Below is a beginner's guide to which
vegetables and herbs are which.

HERBS

Adding fresh herbs to salads
and cooked vegetables lends
extra flavor to them. The
herbs shown here are
the most useful ones to
start with.

Thyme

Bay leaves

Mint

Chives

*Flat-leaf
parsley*

*Curly
parsley*

SALAD LEAVES

You can make green salads
more interesting by trying
out different salad leaves. Use your
favorite lettuce as a base and add
any of the leaves below.

Arugula

Red lettuce

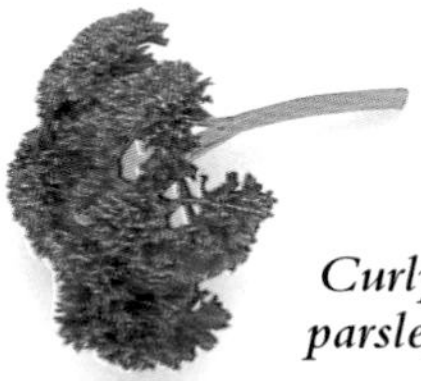

*Romaine
lettuce*

*Curly
endive*

Lambs' lettuce

VEGETABLES

ere are the
getables used in
is book. Buy
em when they
e in season. All
esh vegetables
ould be firm, have
good color, and
free of any marks.

Avocado

Celery

Chinese cabbage

White onion

Yellow onion

Red onion

Garlic

Carrots

Red pepper

Orange pepper

Green pepper

BEANS

You can make wonderful
vegetable stews and
salads with beans. They are
especially good for vegetarians.
Try using canned beans
to start with, because
dried beans take a long
time to cook.

*Red kidney
beans*

*Great Northern
beans*

Pinto beans

Broccoli

Fresh peas

Zucchini

Small cucumber

*Plum
tomato*

*Cherry
tomato*

*Medium
tomato*

Beefsteak tomato

Red potato

New potatoes

53

COOKING VEGETABLES

The key to cooking vegetables is not overcooking them. They should be tender but still have a firm texture. Here is a guide to preparing and cooking some favorite vegetables. To test whether they are cooked, push the point of a knife into one piece.

Cauliflower

Cut the leaves off the cauliflower then cut out the core and cut it into florets. Cook it in boiling salted water for 5 to 6 minutes until just tender, then drain it and season well.

Carrots

Peel big carrots and scrub small ones. Trim the ends off, then slice or cut them into small sticks.

Cook them in boiling salted water for 8 to 10 minutes, then drain and *season* them.

Broccoli

Cut the thick stem off the broccoli and cut it into small, even-sized florets. Cook it in the same way as cauliflower, stem side down in the water, or steam it until tender.

Peas

Take the fresh peas out of their pods and cook them in a little boiling salted water for 5 to 10 minutes. Drain them and add salt, pepper, and a little butter. Frozen peas should be brought to a boil, then *simmered* for 3 to 4 minutes.

Preparing vegetables

1 Wash vegetables in cold water, but do not let them soak. If they are muddy, scrub them with a small brush.

2 Small vegetables only need to be washed, but it is best to peel larger vegetables that have tougher skins.

3 Slice the ends off the vegetables, cut away any tough stalks, or pick off any damaged leaves. Slice them if they are big.

Mushrooms

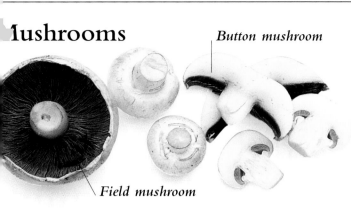

Button mushroom

Field mushroom

Wipe mushrooms clean. Trim the stalks level with the caps and slice the mushrooms vertically. Gently sauté the mushrooms in butter for a few minutes, stirring all the time, until they are tender.

Potatoes

New potato

All-purpose potato

Scrub new potatoes. Peel big potatoes and cut out any eyes (or scrub them, then peel them when cooked). Cook them in boiling salted water for 12 to 18 minutes until tender.

Green beans

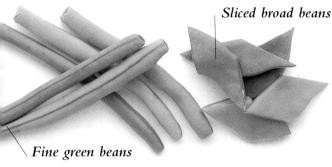

Sliced broad beans

Fine green beans

Trim the ends off fine green beans with a pair of scissors. Cut the ends off broad beans, strip away the stringy edge, and slice them. Boil or steam both kinds of beans for about 5 minutes, until tender.

Zucchini

Zucchini cut into sticks

Sliced zucchini

Wipe zucchini clean, then cut them into thin rounds or slice them into small sticks. Sauté gently in a mixture of butter and oil for 5 to 6 minutes until the edges are crisp and brown.

Cooking vegetables

Bring some salted water to a boil in a saucepan. Add the prepared vegetables and *simmer* them gently until tender.

Steaming vegetables

Cook the vegetables in a steamer over a little boiling water. Keep a lid on the pan until the vegetables are done.

Sautéing vegetables

Heat a pat of butter and a little oil in a skillet and fry the vegetables gently until cooked, stirring them often.

SALAD TIME

Salads can be a light accompaniment to a main course or a meal in themselves. Here you can find out how to make a leafy green side salad and dressing and a main-course Greek salad using the same salad dressing.

You will need (for 4 servings)

For the green salad

Parsley

Chives

½ lb mixed salad greens

For the Greek salad

1 small head of romaine lettuce

1 red onion

1 small cucumber

8–10 pitted black olives

½ lb feta or other sharp, crumbly cheese

4 big tomatoes

For the dressing

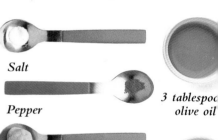
Salt

Pepper

3 tablespoo
olive oil

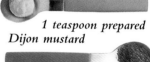
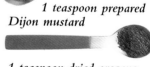
1 teaspoon prepared
Dijon mustard

1 teaspoon dried oregano
(for the Greek salad)

1 tablespo
wine vinega
lemon ju

Green salad

1 Wash and dry the salad greens, then tear them into a salad bowl. *Chop* the herbs and add them to the leaves.

2 Put all the ingredients for the dressing into the jar. Screw on the lid and shake it until everything is mixed together.

3 When you are ready to eat, pour the dressing onto the salad and mix it until the leaves are coated in dressing.

Greek salad

1 Cut the lettuce into *shreds* and put in a salad bowl. Peel and *slice* the onion. Cut the tomatoes into wedges.

2 *Dice* the cucumber. Cut the cheese into cubes. Put the tomatoes, cheese, cucumber, onions, and olives in the bowl.

3 Make a dressing as for the green salad and add the dried oregano. Pour it on the salad and mix everything together well.

Juicy salads

Serve the green salad with grilled meat and fish or before a dish of pasta. The Greek salad makes a wonderful summer meal by itself, served with chunks of crisp bread.

GREEK SALADS

You can use feta cheese or any crumbly cheese with a sharp flavor

Try using different salad leaves, such as leaf lettuce, spinach, and cabbage

GREEN SALAD

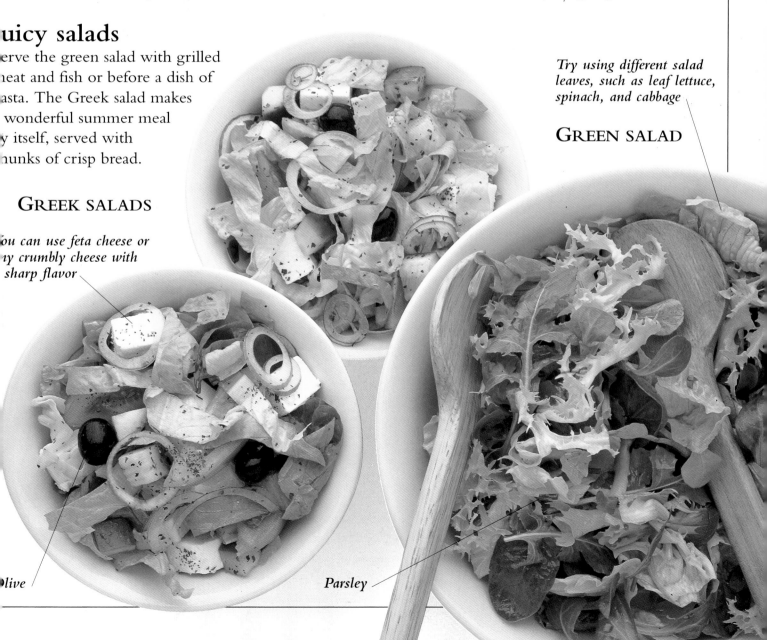

Olive

Parsley

STUFFED POTATOES

Stuffed baked potatoes in their jackets are one of the easiest things to prepare and make a meal in themselves. Here are four different fillings to try. The ingredients shown are enough to fill one potato, so increase them as needed or invent your own fillings.

You will need
(for 4 servings)

4 large potatoes (one per person)

Salt and pepper

Shrimp filling

1 tablespoon yogurt

2 tablespoons chopped cucumber

1/4 cup peeled small shrimp

Cheese filling

1/4 cup grated carrot

1/2 slice of pineapple

1/4 cup grated cheese

Tuna filling

1 tablespoon mayonnaise

2 tablespoons cooked corn

3 tablespoons canned tuna

1 tablespoon chopped scallion

Ham filling

1 slice of chopped ham

1 tablespoon sour cream

1 tablesp chopped c

What to do

1 Set the oven to 400°F. Scrub the potatoes under running water and dry them with a kitchen towel.

2 Prick the potatoes all over with a fork, then wrap them in foil, put them on a baking sheet, and put them in the oven.

3 The potatoes take 1 to 1½ hours to cook. When they are nearly ready, chop and grate the ingredients for the fillings.

A meal in a potato

Eat the potatoes immediately, while hot. They make a filling meal by themselves, or you could serve them with green salad.

HAMMY POTATO

Ham

Chives

CHEESY POTATO

Cheese

Carrot

POTATO WITH SHRIMP

Shrimp

Cucumber

TUNA POTATO

Tuna

Chopped scallion

4 Then put the ingredients for each filling in a bowl and mix them together. Taste it and add salt and pepper if needed.

5 After an hour, take the potatoes out of the oven. Unwrap one and push a knife into it. If it is soft, it is done.

6 Unwrap the potatoes and make cross-shaped cuts in each of them. Spoon the filling into the cuts in the potatoes.

CHEESE AND POTATO BAKE

This delicious recipe is useful as a lunch or supper main dish. Or you can leave out the cheese and use it as a vegetable dish to serve with roast meat or ham. It takes one and a half hours to cook, so allow plenty of time.

You will need (for 4 servings)

1 cup grated Gruyère
or sharp Cheddar cheese

1 egg

Salt

Freshly ground black pepper

2 tablespoons butter

⅔ cup heavy cream

1½ lbs medium to large potatoes

1 large onion

What to do

1 Set the oven to 350°F. Peel the potatoes and *slice* them finely. Put them in a bowl of water.

2 *Slice* the onion finely. Melt the butter in the saucepan over low heat and cook the onion until slightly soft.

3 *Grate* the cheese. Butter the baking dish and spread a layer of sliced potatoes on the bottom. Spoon some onions on top.

4 Add salt and pepper and sprinkle with cheese. Continue layering potatoes, onions, and cheese, finishing with potatoes.

5 *Beat* the egg into the cream with a fork. Pour it over the potatoes and sprinkle the rest of the cheese on top.

6 *Bake* the potatoes for about 1½ hours. Test them with a knife to check that they are cooked all the way through.

Golden and bubbling

This delicious dish is a good thing to make for vegetarian friends. Decorate with a sprig of parsley and serve it with a green vegetable or a tossed salad.

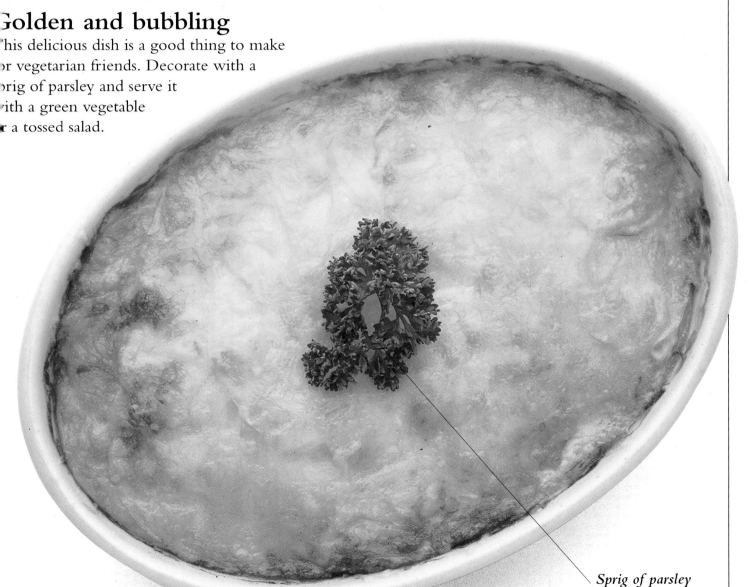

Sprig of parsley

COWBOY BEAN BAKE

Here is a delicious quick version of baked beans. It's made with canned beans, but you could use cooked dried beans instead. You can adapt it for vegetarians by leaving out the bacon and sausages. It is a complete meal in itself.

You will need (for 4 servings)

1 large onion

15oz can crushed tomatoes

2 tablespoons vegetable oil

½ lb hot Italian sausages (or your favorite sausages)

½ lb bacon

1 lb canned or cooked beans (Great Northern, pinto, and/or red kidney beans)

1 tablespoon dark brown sugar

1 teaspoon prepared mustard

A pinch of salt and pepper

COOK'S TOOLS

*Big saucepan • Chopping board
Can opener • Sharp knife
Wooden spoon • Colander*

What to do

1 Peel the onion and slice it finely. Cut the bacon into small cubes. Cut the sausages into chunky slices.

2 Pour the beans into the colander and drain them well. If they had salt and sugar added to them in the can, rinse them.

3 Heat the oil in the saucepan. Cook the onion, bacon, and sausages together until the onion is golden and soft.

4 Add the crushed tomatoes, brown sugar, and mustard and stir. Heat the sauce until it is beginning to bubble.

5 Turn the heat down and let the sauce *simmer* for about half an hour. Stir it now and then to make sure nothing is sticking.

6 Add the drained beans to the sauce and stir everything well. Cook for a few more minutes, until the beans are hot.

Bean feast

Serve the bean bake with chunks of bread to help mop up any leftover sauce.

Red kidney bean

Pinto bean

Onion

Bacon

Italian sausage

Great Northern beans

MEAT AND FISH

Meat and fish are the main ingredients
in this part of the book. You can learn how
to make all sorts of impressive main courses,
from grilled kabobs to a rich beef stew. You
must always make sure the meat or fish is fresh.
Here is a simple guide to the meat and fish
used and the spices that appear
throughout the book.

SPICES

Spices are used to add flavor
to food. You can buy them
already ground or grind your
own in a coffee grinder.

Cinnamon sticks

*Fresh
ginger
root*

Cayenne

Cloves

Ground ginger

Turmeric

Black pepper

Ground cinnamon

Sea salt

Curry powder

Italian seasoning

FISH

You can buy fresh fillets of fish from
fish stores and supermarkets.
Smoked fish has a stronger
flavor than fresh fish. Ask
an adult or the fish store
to skin the fish for you.

*Smoke
haddoc*

Shrimp

Cod fillet

Shrimp add a touch of luxury to
a dish. You can add them to fish
pie, rice casseroles, or sauces. Make sure frozen
shrimp defrost thoroughly before using them.

MEAT

The most common types of red meat are pork, lamb, and beef. In general, the more expensive the meat is, the more tender it will be when cooked. Ask an adult to choose the right meat for you.

Ground beef

GROUND AND CUBED MEAT

Use ground beef to make hamburgers and Bolognese sauce for pasta. Buy meat already cut in cubes for the kabobs and stew.

Pork

Beef

Lamb

CHICKEN

For making the spicy chicken, buy chicken cut into breast pieces and drumsticks. The best meat to use for kabobs is skinned chicken breast.

Chicken drumsticks

Chicken breast

Frankfurter

Bacon

SAUSAGES AND BACON

Bacon is used to add flavor to a lot of dishes. There is a large range of sausages available. Try the different kinds and see which you like the best.

Link sausages

Pork and garlic sausage

Pork and herb sausages

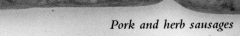

Spicy chorizo sausages

65

HAMBURGER FEAST

Homemade hamburgers taste far better than fast-food ones, and they are really quick and easy to make. Why not experiment with lots of toppings and see whether you can invent a new king-size hamburger?

COOK'S TOOLS

Mixing bowl • Cutting board Pancake turner • Sharp knife • Fork

You will need (for 4 servings)

For the burgers

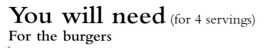

½ onion

1 egg yolk

1 lb ground beef

½ teaspoon salt

½ teaspoon freshly ground black pepper

4 sesame seed hamburger buns

For the toppings

Mayonnaise

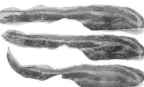

Sliced cheese

Cooked slices of bacon

Sliced tomatoes

Sliced onion

Lettuce leaves

What to do

1 Peel and finely *chop* the onion for the hamburgers. Slice the tomatoes and the onion rings for the garnishes.

2 Put the ground beef, egg yolk, chopped onion, salt, and pepper in the mixing bowl and mix them together well.

3 Divide the hamburger mixture into four even-size pieces and roll each one into a ball with the palm of your hand.

4 Then flatten each of the balls into a round patty. Firm the edges of the hamburgers to give them a good shape.

5 Heat the grill until hot, then *grill* the hamburgers on each side for 5 to 10 minutes, until firm and brown.

6 Put each hamburger in a bun. Then put sliced tomatoes, cheese, bacon, onion, or lettuce on top and add mayonnaise.

All in a burger

Arrange the toppings carefully so they don't spill out of the burgers. Serve the burgers with ketchup, mustard, or pickle relish.

SALAD BURGER

Mayonnaise

Burger

Sliced onion

Lettuce

Sliced tomato

BACON BURGER

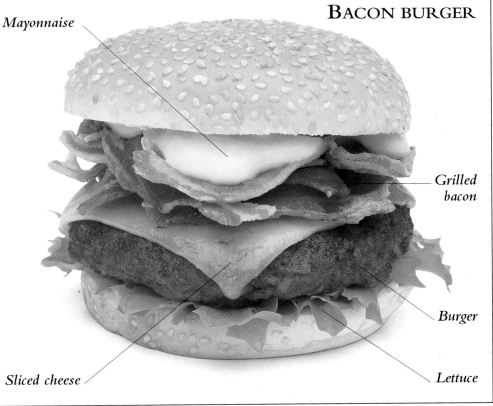

Mayonnaise

Grilled bacon

Burger

Sliced cheese

Lettuce

KABOBS

Kabobs are grilled skewers of meat and vegetables. They are great for barbecues. Here you can see how to make sausage, chicken, and lamb kabobs as well as how to marinate, or soak, the meat in a sauce first to make it really tender.

You will need (for 3 kabobs)

For the marinade

Black pepper

½ onion

⅔ cup olive oil

1 lemon

For the sausage kabob

2 cherry tomatoes

2 button mushrooms

3 small sausages

For the chicken kabob

1 small zucchini

4 cubes of chicken breast

¼ red pepper

For the lamb kabob

¼ green pepper

4 cubes of lamb

2 small onions

2 dried apricots

Marinating meat

1 *Chop* the onion very finely. Cut the lemon in half and squeeze out the juice with the lemon squeezer.

2 Put the onion, lemon juice, olive oil, and black pepper in the shallow dish and mix them together with a spoon.

3 Lay the cubes of meat in the mixture (*marinade*) and leave them to soak for a few hours, turning them now and then.

Making the kabobs

1 When you are ready to cook, prepare the vegetables. Cut the peppers into cubes and the zucchini into short pieces.

2 Drain the meat, then push the chosen ingredients tightly onto the skewers. Be careful of the skewers' sharp points.

3 Preheat the grill, then *grill* the kabobs for about 10 minutes. Turn them once or twice so they cook all over.

A meal on a skewer

You can put together any ingredients you like for kabobs. Mix different meats and vegetables and choose colors as well as flavors that go well together.

LAMB KABOB

Cube of green pepper

Small onion

Apricot

Cube of lamb

SAUSAGE KABOB

Cherry tomato

Mushroom

Small sausage

CHICKEN KABOB

Cube of chicken

Cube of red pepper

Zucchini

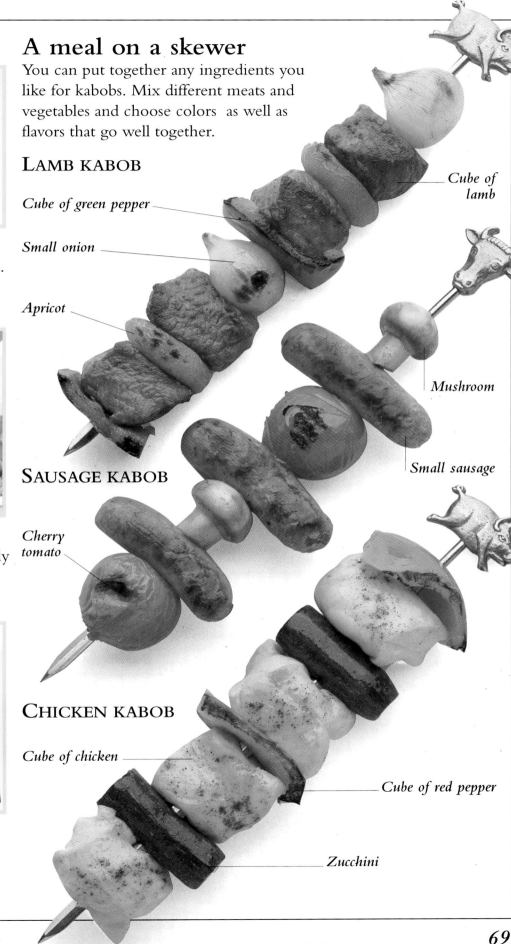

SPICY CHICKEN

This wonderful recipe has a truly exotic flavor, created by a colorful mixture of spices. Allow a couple of hours to prepare the chicken, because it has to marinate, or soak, in a spicy sauce for an hour before you cook it, to make it tender.

COOK'S TOOLS

Large bowl • Cutting board
Sharp knife • Fork • Skillet
Garlic press • Spoon
Wooden spoon • Baking sheet

You will need (for 4 servings)

4 chicken portions, each cut in half

1 cup plain yogurt

1½ tablespoons vegetable oil

1 large onion

Small clove garlic

Salt and pepper

1 teaspoon turmeric

1 teaspoon curry powder

¼ teaspoon cayenne pepper

What to do

1 Put the pieces of chicken on the cutting board and make two deep cuts across each of them with a sharp knife.

2 Mix half of the spices and a tablespoon of oil in the bowl. Add the chicken and turn it. Leave it to *marinate* for an hour.

3 Set the oven to 350°F. Put the chicken pieces on the baking sheet and *bake* them for 30 minutes.

4 *Chop* the onion. Heat the rest of the oil in the skillet and fry the onion gently until soft and golden.

5 Mix the rest of the spices and garlic into the yogurt until creamy. Add the fried onions and stir everything together.

6 Spoon the mixture on top of the pieces of chicken. Then bake them for 20 to 30 minutes more, until golden brown.

Eastern flavor

Serve the chicken on a bed of plain cooked rice (see page 46) and garnish it with sprigs of fresh coriander (cilantro).

Coriander

71

BEEF STEW

This rich stew will really impress your family and friends, yet it doesn't take long to prepare. The secret of its success is that it has to be cooked slowly for quite a long time. This makes the meat very tender and gives the sauce a lot of flavor.

You will need (for 4 servings)

1½ lb beef stew meat,
cut into cubes

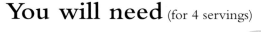

3 slices of bacon

2 onions

1 clove garlic

1¾ cups beef stock

2 carrots

A few strips of orange peel

A large pinch of Italian seasoning

2 tablespoons vegetable oil

2 tablespoons chopped parsley

1 tablespoon all–purpose flour

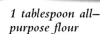

1 tablespoon tomato puree

Salt

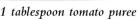

Pepper

What to do

1 Set the oven to 350°F. *Chop* the onions and bacon with a sharp knife, slice the carrots, and *crush* the garlic.

2 Mix the flour, salt, and pepper on the plate. Lay the meat on top and turn it until each piece is coated with flour.

3 Heat 1 tablespoon oil in the casserole and fry the carrots and onions for a few minutes. Remove with a slotted spoon.

4 Heat the rest of the oil in the casserole dish, then add the meat and stir it as it cooks until it lightly browned all over.

5 Return the vegetables to the casserole dish with the meat. Add the tomato puree, garlic, herbs, and orange peel and stir.

6 Add the stock and stir. Then put the lid on the casserole and cook it for about two hours, until the meat is tender.

Meal in a pot

The finished stew is rich and smooth. Sprinkle it with chopped parsley and serve it with baked, boiled, or mashed potatoes and a green vegetable.

Chopped parsley

FISHERMAN'S PIE

This is a warming dish that is good for cold days. It will also teach you two useful cook's skills: how to mash potatoes and how to make a white sauce. You can vary the recipe by using different types of fish or by adding ¼ lb peeled shrimp.

You will need (for 4 servings)

2 lb potatoes

½ cup all–purpose flour

½ cup grated cheese

6 tablespoons butter

2 hard-boiled eggs

Parsley

1 lb smoked fish

1 lb white fish

2 ⅔ cups milk

Pepper

Salt

What to do

1 Set the oven to 400°F. Peel the potatoes and put them in a saucepan of water to boil.

2 Meanwhile, cut the fish into chunks about 1 inch square. *Chop* the peeled hard-boiled eggs and the parsley.

3 Then make a white sauce. Melt 4 tablespoons butter in a saucepan. Add the flour and st it until it forms a thick paste.

4 Gradually stir the milk into the mixture. Cook over low eat, stirring it as it thickens. dd parsley, salt, and pepper.

5 When the potatoes have cooked, drain them and mash them. Stir in the rest of the butter, a little milk, and salt and pepper.

6 Put the fish and chopped egg in the dish. Pour the sauce over them. Spoon the potato on top and sprinkle with cheese.

Hot from the oven

Bake the pie for about 30 minutes, ntil the potato topping is an even olden brown and crisp around the dges. Serve it with a green vegetable, ach as broccoli or peas.

Parsley garnish

Potato topping

Parsley sauce

Fish

COOKIES, BREADS, AND CAKES

Home baking is great fun. You can create all kinds
of delicious treats, from gingerbread folk and
fresh bread rolls to impressive iced cakes. This section
of the book is full of basic recipes for cookies,
breads, and cakes which you can vary in different ways.
Here are the main ingredients you will be using.

DRIED FRUIT

Dried fruit and glacé cherries are mainly
added to cakes. Rinse the syrup off glacé
cherries before using them.

SWEETENERS

Granulated sugar is good for most
cakes, meringues, and cookies. Bro[...]
sugar and molasses have a stronger
taste and are good with whole-wh[...]
flour or in fruit cakes. Honey can
also be used as a sweetener, where
specified. Confectioners' sugar, a
very fine sugar, is used to
make icing.

Apricots

Glacé cherries

Raisins

Golden raisins (sultanas)

Currants

Brown sugar

YEAST AND BAKING POWDER

Yeast is added to bread and baking powder to cakes to make them rise when baked. The easiest yeast to use is quick-rise dried yeast, which you just sprinkle onto the flour. Baking powder is added to all-purpose flour for cakes.

Soft margarine

FATS AND OILS

Butter has the best flavor for making cakes and cookies, but margarine is also good. Soft margarine is used for packaged cake mixes. Pastry is best made with a mixture of butter and lard or vegetable shortening. Vegetable oil is added to bread dough. Sunflower oil has a good mild flavor.

Fresh yeast   *Quick-rise dried yeast*   *Baking powder*

Butter

FLOUR

All-purpose white or whole-wheat flour is best for cakes and pastries. If using white flour, look for unbleached flour. Use bread or whole-wheat flour for making bread. Self-rising flour has baking powder added to it.

Lard or vegetable shortening

Vegetable oil

Unbleached all-purpose white flour

All-purpose white flour

Whole-wheat flour

Honey   *Granulated sugar*   *Confectioners' sugar*   *Dark brown sugar*

GINGERBREAD FOLK

You can cut these spicy gingerbread cookies into people, trees, stars, and other shapes, then decorate them with icing. Here you can find out how to make the cookies and on pages 80 to 81 you can see how to decorate them.

You will need (for about 30 cookies)

on pages 80 to 81

COOK'S TOOLS

Baking sheets • Rolling pin
Wooden spoon • Pastry brush
Spatula • Knife • Spoon • Fork
Cookie cutters • Small bowl
Mixing bowl • Wire rack
Saucepan • Strainer • Toothpick

3 cups
all-purpose flour

1/4 lb (1 stick) butter

2 teaspoons
ground ginger

A few currants
or raisins

1 teaspoon baking soda

1 beaten egg

1/4 cup golden syrup or honey

7/8 cup packed brown sugar

What to do

1 Set the oven to 375°F. Melt a little of the butter nd *grease* the baking sheets using pastry brush.

2 Put the butter, sugar, and syrup in a saucepan and stir them together over low heat until they have melted.

3 *Sift* the flour, ground ginger, and baking soda into the mixing bowl. Add the syrup mixture and the beaten egg.

4 Mix everything together and *knead* it into a ball. Chill he dough in a plastic bag in the efrigerator for 30 minutes.

5 Sprinkle some flour on the table and rolling pin. Then *roll the dough out* until it is about ¼ inch thick.

6 Use the cookie cutters or a knife to cut out the people and other shapes. Press the cutters down, then lift them off.

7 Lift the cookies onto the baking sheet. Then gather p the leftover dough, roll it out gain, and cut out more shapes.

8 Make holes with a toothpick in the top of any cookies you want to hang up. Press currant eyes and buttons into the people.

9 *Bake* the cookies for 10 to 15 minutes, until they are golden brown, then transfer them to a wire rack to cool.

ICING COOKIES

We have piped white, green, and red icing onto the cookies to decorate them. To make the leaf cookies, mark the veins with a knife while the cookies are still uncooked. Let the other cookies cool completely before icing them.

You will need

(for 30 cookies)

Small amount of water

Several drops of green food coloring

Several drops of red food coloring

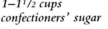

1–1 1/2 cups confectioners' sugar

Narrow, colored ribbons

What to do

1 Sift the confectioners' sugar into the bowl. Add a little water at a time into the sugar to make a thick, smooth paste.

2 Spoon a quarter of the icing into each of the two smaller bowls and add food coloring to it to make green and red icing.

3 Fill the *pastry bags* with the green, red, and white icing and pipe it carefully onto the cookies to make patterns.

Pretty as pictures

Why not try making a gingerbread family or your own Christmas tree decorations? Thread ribbon through the holes in the cookies to tie them to the tree.

HOLLY LEAVES

FANCY STAR

POLKA DOT COOKIES

CHRISTMAS TREE

STAR

GINGERBREAD FAMILY

CHOCOLATE CHIP COOKIES

Here's a quick and easy recipe for some really popular cookies. The quantities given here will make about 18 cookies. You can vary them by adding 1 cup of chopped walnuts if you like.

You will need (for about 18 cookies)

1/3 cup sugar

1/4 lb (1 stick) softened butter

1 1/4 cups all-purpose flour

1 egg

1/2 teaspoon baking soda

1/2 teaspoon vanilla extract

1/4 teaspoon salt

A 6-oz bag of chocolate chips

1/3 cup packed brown sugar

What to do

1 Set the oven to 375°F. *Beat* the butter together with both kinds of sugar in a mixing bowl until creamy.

2 Break the egg into the bowl and beat it into the mixture until smooth. Then add the vanilla extract and mix it in.

3 Add the flour, salt, and baking soda to the mixture a little at a time. Stir everything together until smooth.

4 Now add the chocolate chips and stir them in until they are spread evenly through the cookie dough.

5 Butter the baking sheets and spoon small mounds of the dough onto them, leaving lots of space between the mounds.

6 *Bake* the cookies for 10 to 12 minutes, until they are an even golden brown, then transfer them to a wire rack to cool.

Chocolate chip cookies

Once the cookies are completely cool, store them in an airtight container to keep them crisp and fresh.

The cookies should be crisp on the outside and slightly soft in the center.

Chocolate chip

BAKING BREAD

There is something magical about making bread and watching it rise, yet it is very easy. This recipe will make a medium-sized plain or chocolate loaf and about eight rolls. Turn the page to see how to shape the rolls into lots of fun shapes.

You will need

1 tablespoon sunflower oil

2 teaspoons salt

1 3/4 cups warm water

1 1/4-oz envelope quick-rise yeast

6 cups whole-wheat or bread flour

Sunflower seeds *Sesame seeds*

For chocolate loaf

4 1/2 tablespoons sugar

3/4 cup unsweetened cocoa powder

What to do

1 Put the flour, salt, yeast (and sugar and cocoa powder if you are making the chocolate bread) in the bowl.

2 Add the sunflower oil and water and stir everything together with a wooden spoon until you have a soft *dough*.

3 Sprinkle some flour on the table. *Knead* the dough on it for about five minutes, until it is smooth and elastic.

Loaf in a pan

Shape half the dough into a loaf and press it into an oiled pan. Cover with a kitchen towel. Put in a warm place for 40 minutes.

Shaping a round loaf

Roll half the dough into a ball and put it on a baking sheet. *Score* it with a knife, cover it with a kitchen towel, and let it rise.

Baking the loaf

Set the oven to 425°F. Put the loaf in the heated oven when it has risen to double its size. *Bake* it for 35 minutes.

Warm from the oven

If the bread is not quite ready, bake it for a little longer. It is done when it sounds hollow if you tap it underneath. Once done, put it on a wire rack to cool. Bread is easier to slice when it is completely cool.

Chocolate bread tastes savory rather than sweet and is good with cream cheese. This bread was shaped into a round loaf and scored on top.

WHITE BREAD

This classic white bread was baked in a loaf pan. It has been decorated with pumpkin seeds. Any seeds should be sprinkled on top of the bread after it has risen, but before it is put in the oven to bake.

CHOCOLATE BREAD

85

FUNNY ROLLS

Try making rolls with the rest of the bread dough. They will take about 20 minutes to rise. Brush them with milk if adding seeds. They are done when golden.

Shaping the rolls

Set the oven to 425°F. Break the dough into eight pieces the same size and then roll them into small balls.

Flat bread

For a mini-loaf, shape one of the balls into a loaf and put it in a greased pan. For an herb bread, flatten the balls into circles.

You will need

For herb bread topping

A sprig of rosemary

1 clove of garlic

1 tablespoon sea salt

1 tablespoon vegetable oil

For decorating mini-loaves

Currants or raisins

Sesame seeds

Poppy seeds

Cracked wheat

KNOT ROLL

Sesame seeds

HERB BREAD

Add oil, garlic, rosemary, and salt on top

MINI WHITE LOAF

Poppy seeds

Rolling dough

o make knots, pretzels, and nails, start by rolling each ball f dough into a long thin ausage shape with your hands.

Knots and pretzels

Fold each sausage into the shape you want. Make a spiral for a snake and tie a sausage in a loose knot to make a knot roll.

Decorating

Lay the rolls on an oiled baking sheet and decorate them. Let them rise until twice as big, then bake them for 15 minutes.

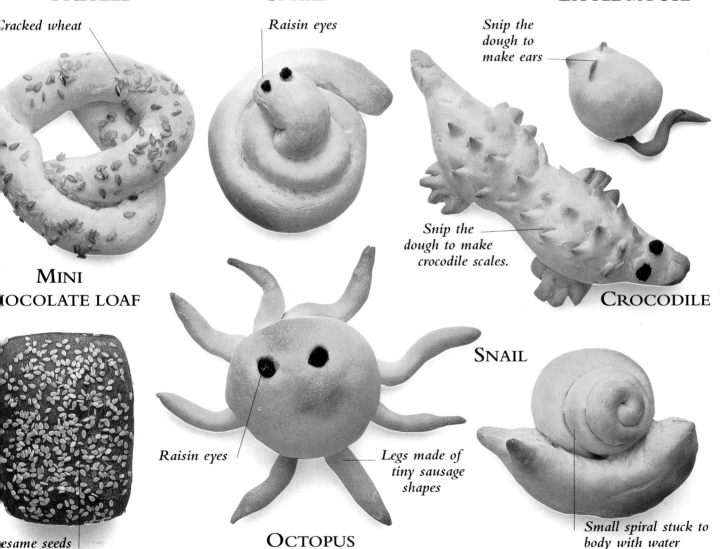

PRETZEL

Cracked wheat

SNAKE

Raisin eyes

LITTLE MOUSE

Snip the dough to make ears

Snip the dough to make crocodile scales.

CROCODILE

MINI CHOCOLATE LOAF

SNAIL

Raisin eyes

Legs made of tiny sausage shapes

Sesame seeds

OCTOPUS

Small spiral stuck to body with water

CUPCAKES

Why not make some cupcakes for dessert? This recipe is for a basic sponge cake mixture which you can vary by adding cherries and coconut or golden raisins. The quantities will make 16 cupcakes and 12 tiny ones. Turn the page for ideas on decoration.

You will need (for 28 cupcakes)

COOK'S TOOLS

*Knife • Muffin pans • Mixing bowl
Small bowl • Paper baking cups
and candy cups • Wooden spoon
Big spoon • Teaspoon
Fork • Wire rack*

1 cup self-rising flour

2 medium-sized eggs

*¹/₂ cup plus
1 tablespoon sugar*

*¹/₄ lb (1 stick)
softened butter*

For raisin cake

²/₃ cup golden raisins

For coconut cake

1 cup flaked coconut

²/₃ cup glacé cherries

What to do

1 Set the oven to 375°F. Put the paper baking cups in one pan and the paper candy cups in the other pan.

2 Cut up the butter and put it in the mixing bowl with the sugar. *Beat* the butter and sugar together until light and creamy.

3 Beat the eggs in a bowl with the fork. Add them to the butter mixture a little at a time using the wooden spoon.

4 Add the flour to the mixture a little at a time and *fold* it in gently. Add the raisins or chopped cherries and coconut if you want.

5 Spoon the cake mixture into the paper cups. *Bake* the tiny cupcakes for 10 minutes and the larger ones for 15 to 20 minutes.

6 The cupcakes are done when they are firm and golden brown. Transfer them from the pans onto a wire rack to cool.

Assorted cupcakes

The finished cupcakes are perfect for company. Why not decorate the plain ones for a special party? Turn the page to see what to do.

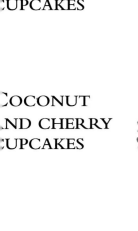

PLAIN CUPCAKES

COCONUT AND CHERRY CUPCAKES

RAISIN CUPCAKES

TINY CUPCAKES

ICING CUPCAKES

For a special occasion it is fun to decorate the cup-cakes. Here we have used colored icing with white piping. Mix the coloring into the icing a drop at a time until it is the right color. Find out how to make pastry bags and do piping in the glossary (see page 126).

(see page 126)

COOK'S TOOLS

Mixing bowl • Pastry bag
4 small bowls • 4 teaspoons
Strainer • Wooden spoon

You will need (for about 28 cupcakes)

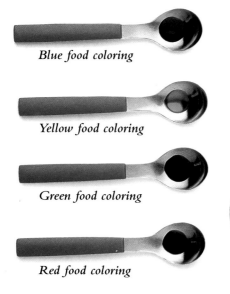

Blue food coloring

Yellow food coloring

Green food coloring

Red food coloring

Confectioners' sugar

Water

Narrow colored ribbons

Coated chocolate candies

What to do

1 Make the icing (see page 80). Spoon a little icing into the four small bowls and stir a few drops of coloring into each one.

2 Put a little colored icing on each cupcake and spread it out evenly to the edges of the cake with the back of a teaspoon.

3 Let the colored icing dry, then fill the *pastry bag* with white icing and *pipe* patterns on top of the cupcakes.

Up, up, and away!

Why not ice the bigger cupcakes to look like balloons? Tuck ribbons under them to look like swirling strings. Decorate the tiny cupcakes with candies in contrasting colors.

Lines piped in white icing

Coated chocolate candy

ICED SPONGE CAKE

This wonderful all-in-one cake is incredibly easy to make. You can flavor it with orange, lemon, or chocolate. Repeat the recipe to make a second layer. Use chocolate icing for the filling in the middle and the coating on top.

You will need (for one layer of cake)

1/4 lb (1 stick)
softened margarine

2 large eggs

1/2 cup plus 1 tablespoon
sugar

2–3 drops vanilla extract

A pinch of salt

1 cup self-rising flour

1 teaspoon baking powder

COOK'S TOOLS

Wire rack • 2 circles of wax paper
7 inches across • 2 x 7-inch layer cake
pans • Mixing bowl • Pastry brush
Wooden spoon • Spatula

For icing the cakes

Heatproof bowl • Saucepan
Wooden spoon

For lemon cake

Grated zest of
a lemon
1 tablespoon
lemon juice

For orange cake

Grated zest of
an orange
1 tablespoon
orange juice

For chocolate cake

6 tablespoons sifted
unsweetened cocoa
powder, to replace same
amount of flour

Chocolate topping and filling

4 oz milk chocolate

2 tablespoons
sour cream

White chocolate topping and filling

6 oz white chocolate

2 tablespoons
sour cream

What to do

1 Set the oven to 325°F. Put all the ingredients for the cake you are making in the mixing bowl.

2 Mix all the ingredients together with the wooden spoon, then *beat* the mixture hard for about two minutes.

3 The cake mixture should drop off a spoon easily. If it seems too stiff, stir in two teaspoons of water and beat it again.

Icing the cakes

4 Divide the mixture between two *greased* and *lined* cake pans and smooth it level. *Bake* the cakes for 30 minutes, until firm.

5 Slide a spatula around the edges of the pans to loosen the cakes and turn them out onto a wire rack. Remove the wax paper.

1 Break the chocolate up into a small bowl. Add the sour cream. Heat a saucepan of water over low heat.

2 Place the bowl on top of the saucepan of water. Stir the chocolate and sour cream together until the chocolate has melted.

3 When the cakes are cool, turn one of them upside down and spread half of the chocolate icing on it with a spatula.

4 Put the other cake on top of the icing, then spread the rest of the icing smoothly on top and sides of the layer cake.

CAKE DECORATING

The best part of making a cake is decorating it! Wait for the icing to set, then gather your decorations together and work out how to arrange them on a large plate. You can copy the cakes here or try out ideas of your own. If you don't have these ingredients, use something similar.

You will need (for 4 cakes)

Cutters for making different shapes

White chocolate chips

Red licorice strings (or use red icing)

White fondant icing or marzipan

Red fondant icing or marzipan

Sliced almonds

FUNNY FAC

Sliced almonds

Sprinkles

White chocolate chips

Dark chocolate chips

Glacé cherries

Coated chocolate candies

Chocolate-dipped fruit (see page 101)

FRUIT FIESTA

Chocolate-dipped strawberry

Chocolate-dipped grape

Glacé cherry

Chocolate-dipped mandarin orange segment

Glacé cherry nose

Coated chocolate candies

Numbers cut out of red fondant icing

Hands cut out of white fondant icing

CLOCK CAKE

Eyes made with chocolate chips and candies

Red licorice strings or red icing

Mouth filled in with sprinkles

White chocolate chips

95

DESSERTS AND TREATS

The desserts in this part of the book are
based on fruit and chocolate and range from
scrumptious chocolate-dipped fruit to hot apple pie.
While making them you can also learn useful basic
skills, such as how to make pastry, meringues,
and crêpe batter. Here is a quick guide
to the key ingredients.

NUTS

Nuts go really well with both
fruit and chocolate. You will
find them in the baking
section of a supermarket.
For extra flavor and
crunchiness, toast them in the
oven (ask an adult to help).

Hazelnuts

CHOCOLATE

Look for chocolate with
a high percentage of
cocoa solids (check the
package). More expensive
types of chocolate taste
better and melt more easily.

*Chocolate
wafers*

Chocolate chips

Walnuts

*Blanched (skinned)
almonds*

*Milk
chocolate*

White chocolate

*Dark
chocolate*

FRUIT

Choose fresh fruit for desserts whenever possible. Fruit should be a good color, firm, and not have any marks on it. Otherwise use fruit that has been canned in natural fruit juices. Some frozen fruits are also good. Allow them to defrost before using them.

CREAM AND YOGURT

Use heavy cream or whipping cream for whipping. Light cream or half-and-half are better for pouring. Yogurt is somewhat sharp, thick, and creamy.

Yogurt

Light cream

Raspberries

Cherries

Strawberries

Pineapple ring

Banana

Red plum

Green grapes

Red grapes

Orange

Plum

Green apple

Red apple

Green pear

Red pear

ICE CREAM SAUCES

You can make ice cream even more scrumptious by serving it with different-flavored sauces. Here are three quick and easy sauces that can transform an ordinary dessert into something really special.

You will need (for 4 servings of each)

For chocolate sauce

4 oz semisweet chocolate

²/₃ cup water

²/₃ cup heavy cream

2 teaspoons superfine sugar

For raspberry sauce

2 tablespoons heavy cream

¹/₄ cup confectioners' sugar

A 10-oz package frozen raspberries

For hot cherry sauce

A 15-oz can red cherries in syrup

2 teaspoons cornstarch

Hot cherry sauce

1 Set the strainer over the bowl and pour the opened can of cherries into it so that the syrup drains into the bowl beneath.

2 Pour the syrup into the saucepan, then *pit* the cherries and put them in the saucepan with the syrup.

3 Mix the cornstarch into a paste with some of the syrup, then stir it into the pan and gently heat the sauce until it thickens.

Chocolate sauce

1 Break the chocolate into pieces into the saucepan, then add the heavy cream, the sugar, and the water.

2 Heat the mixture until it *simmers* and the chocolate melts. Let it simmer for five minutes, *whisking* all the time.

Raspberry sauce

Put the raspberries, sugar, and cream in the *blender* and whiz for about 30 seconds, until everything is mixed together.

All on a sundae

Try the sauces out with different ice creams to find out which combinations you like best. Mix raspberry with chocolate or hot cherry with strawberry. Delicious!

CHERRY DREAM

Hot cherry sauce

Strawberry ice cream

Chocolate sauce

Banana cut in half lengthwise

Vanilla ice cream

BANANA SPLIT

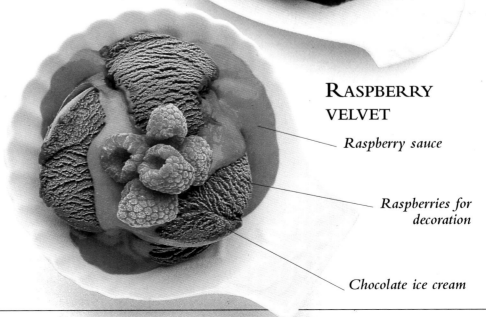

RASPBERRY VELVET

Raspberry sauce

Raspberries for decoration

Chocolate ice cream

CHOCOLATE TREATS

Here are some delicious nibbles for you to try – mini-florentines and chocolate-dipped fruit. You will need to allow at least one hour for the chocolate to set when making them. A 4-oz bar of chocolate will make eight mini-florentines.

You will need (for 4 people)

Good-quality white chocolate

Good-quality milk chocolate

Mixed nuts

Glacé cherries

Golden or dark raisins

Dried apricots

Green grapes

Strawberries

Tangerine segments

Mini-florentines

1 Break the chocolate up into the two bowls. Put the white chocolate in one bowl and the milk chocolate in the other.

2 Heat water in a saucepan and set each bowl on top of it, one at a time, over low heat. Stir the chocolate until it has melted.

3 Put the wax paper on the plate and drop teaspoons of milk and white melted chocolate onto it.

Chocolate dips

4 Chop the cherries and dried
apricots, then arrange the
uit and nuts on the chocolate
d put it in a cool place to set.

1 Dip strawberries, grapes, and
tangerine segments halfway
into the melted chocolate, then
lay them on the wax paper.

2 Put the treats in a cool place
for one to two hours, until
the chocolate is hard. Then peel
them gently off the paper.

asty treats

rrange the mini-florentines
d chocolate-dipped fruits
a pretty pattern on a
ate. Store in a cool
lace, but not in
e refrigerator.

Mini-florentine

Chocolate-dipped
angerine segment

Chocolate-dipped
strawberry

Chocolate-
dipped grape

101

NO-BAKE FRUITCAKE

This scrumptious cross between a cake and a giant cookie can be eaten as dessert or as a special-occasion snack. The clever thing about it is that you don't have to cook it in the oven but just put it in the refrigerator until it is firm.

You will need (for 1 cake)

1/3 cup glacé cherries

2 tablespoons heavy cream

4 oz semisweet chocolate

1 x 8-oz package digestive crackers or graham crackers

2/3 cup sliced almonds

2 1/2 tablespoons raisins

1/4 lb (1 stick) butter

What to do

1 *Line* the cake pan with a large piece of foil. Press the foil carefully into the pan, being careful not to tear it.

2 Chop the cherries. Put the crackers in the mixing bowl and break them up into small pieces. Add the cherries.

3 Break the chocolate into the saucepan. Add the butter and cream and stir over low heat until the chocolate has melted.

4 Add the raisins and almonds to the cracker mixture, then pour in the chocolate sauce. Stir everything together well.

5 Spoon the mixture into the cake pan and press the cherries on top. Cover the cake with foil and press it down firmly.

6 Put the cake in the refrigerator for two hours, until it has set hard. Then lift it out of the pan and peel off the foil.

The finished cake

This cake is so rich that it is best to cut it into small pieces. It should be big enough for eight to ten pieces. People can always have second helpings—if there is any left.

Glacé cherries

Raisin

Sliced almonds

FRUIT TARTS

You can make mouth-watering fruit tarts really easily by using ready-made puff pastry. The secret is to slice the fruit thinly and to arrange it attractively. The quantities below will make three tarts and two banana moons.

You will need (for 5 fruit tarts)

COOK'S TOOLS

Cutting board • Wire rack
Teaspoon • Pastry brush • Sharp knife
Baking sheet • Rolling pin

A sprinkling of superfine sugar

Some melted butter

2 plums

A candied cherry

¹/₂ lb ready-made puff pastry

Warmed, strained apricot jam

A pear

Peeled, sliced peaches

A banana

What to do

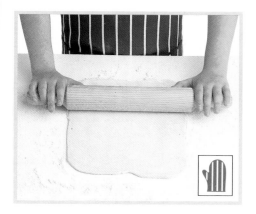

1 Set the oven to 425°F. *Roll* the pastry out on a floured surface using a rolling pin until it is about ¹/₈ in thick.

2 Cut circles out of the pastry around a dish or lid. Then cut around a banana twice to make two banana shapes.

3 *Slice* the plums and pear. Then brush the pastry with the melted butter and arrange slices of fruit on the circles.

4 Cut the banana in half and lay it on the pastry bananas. Brush the prepared fruit with butter and sprinkle sugar on top.

5 Bake the tarts for 20 minutes, until the pastry is crisp and the fruit cooked. Put them on a wire rack to cool.

6 When the tarts have cooled, brush the fruit with a little melted, strained apricot jam to *glaze* the tarts.

Fun fruit tarts

These crisp tarts make delicious desserts. Serve them alone or with a spoonful of cream.

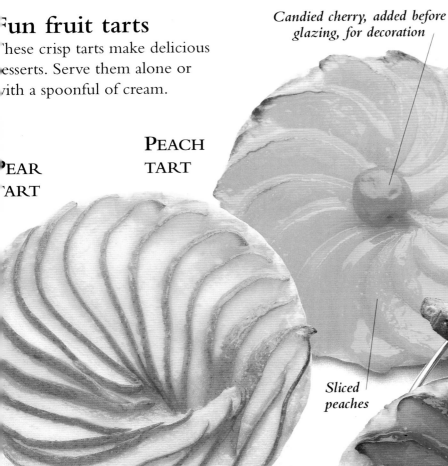

Candied cherry, added before glazing, for decoration

PEAR TART

PEACH TART

BANANA MOON

Glazed half of a banana

Sliced peaches

Thinly sliced pears, arranged in a spiral

PLUM TART

FRUIT IN THE OVEN

Baked apples and bananas are wonderful cold-weather desserts, and they are one of the easiest things to prepare. Add a little butter, sugar, and a sprinkling of golden raisins and just bake them in the oven until they are deliciously soft.

COOK'S TOOLS

Ovenproof baking dish
Cutting board • Lemon squeezer
Bowl • Grater • Apple corer
Teaspoon • Sharp knife

You will need (for 6 servings)

For baked bananas

2 bananas

1 tablespoon light brown sugar

1 tablespoon butter

1/2 of an orange

1 tablespoon golden raisins

For baked apples

2 tablespoons honey

2 tablespoons water

4 big apples

1/3 cup golden or dark raisins

A pinch of ground cinnamon

2 tablespoons butter

2 tablespoons brown sugar

Baked apples

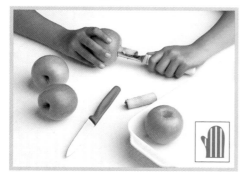

1 Set the oven to 375°F. Make a cut around the middle of each apple and then *core* it.

2 Mix the raisins, sugar, and cinnamon together in a bowl, then spoon the mixture into the hole in each apple.

3 Put a cube of butter on each apple and pour the honey and water on top. *Bake* the apple for 40 minutes or until soft.

aked bananas

1 Set the oven to 425°F. Grate the zest of the orange, en squeeze out the juice. utter the dish.

2 Peel the bananas, cut them in half lengthwise and lay them in the dish. Sprinkle them with orange zest and juice.

3 Put a cube of butter on each banana and sprinkle sugar and raisins on top. Bake them for 10 to 12 minutes until soft.

Hot from the oven

ou can eat the apples and nanas on their own or rve them with fresh eam or custard (see ges 110 and 113).

BAKED APPLE

ut each apple on its wn plate or bowl with spoonful of the warm ney juices.

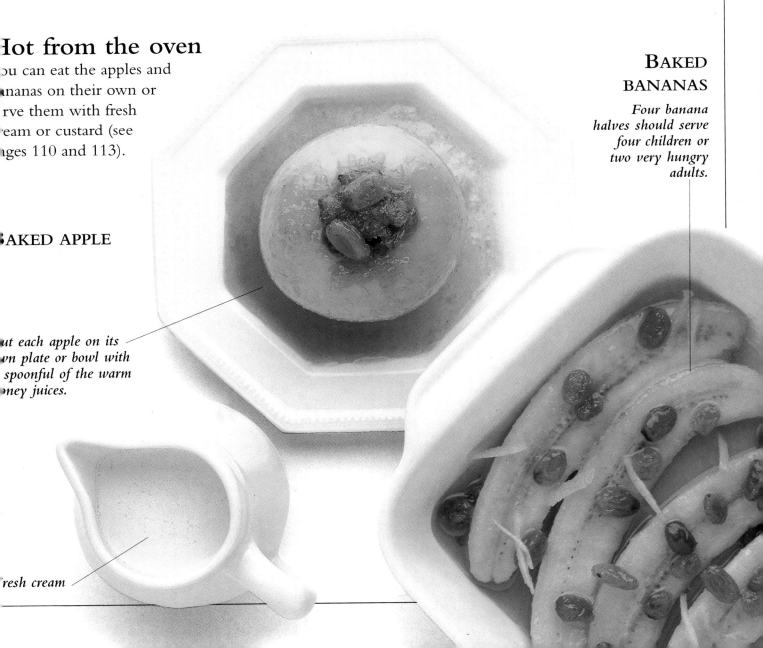

BAKED BANANAS

Four banana halves should serve four children or two very hungry adults.

resh cream

FRUIT BASKETS

These delicious desserts are meringue baskets filled with fresh cream and topped with fruit. The key to good meringue is to cook it at a low temperature until it is really dry. So allow a couple of hours for cooking to make it really perfect.

Baking sheet • Nonstick baking parchment • Mixing bowl • Wire rack Cutting board • Sharp knife Teaspoon • Small bowl • Whisk

You will need (for 6 meringues)

A pinch of salt

Any fruit you like

Black and green grapes

A sprig of mint

Raspberries

Strawberries

2 egg whites

²/₃ *cup heavy cream or whipping cream*

¹/₂ *cup plus 1 tablespoon superfine sugar*

Sliced peaches

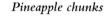

Canned mandarin oranges

Pineapple chunks

What to do

1 Set the oven to 250°F. Line the baking sheet with a piece of nonstick baking parchment or waxed paper.

2 Pour the egg whites into the mixing bowl. Add the salt and *whisk* them together until the egg whites form stiff peaks.

3 Add the sugar, a little at a time, and keep whisking until all the sugar has been mixed into the egg whites.

4 Spoon small mounds of the mixture onto the baking sheet. Then *bake* them for about two hours, until they are dry.

5 Whisk the cream until it is thick. Pick the stalks off the strawberries and cut all the fruit into slices or small pieces.

6 Spoon whipped cream onto the meringues, then arrange the sliced fruit on top to look like flower petals.

CARNATION
Pineapple chunk
Sliced strawberry

ROSE
Raspberry

POPPY
Green grape
Strawberry half

PANSY
Mint leaves
Sliced peach
Raspberry

ORCHID
Black grape
Canned mandarin orange

DAFFODIL
Raspberry
Half a slice of peach

APPLE PIE AND CUSTARD

Here you can find out how to make a deep-dish pie. You can make it with apples or any other fruit you like – the choice is yours! Turn the page to see how to decorate the pie and make a yummy custard to pour over the top.

You will need (for one pie)

COOK'S TOOLS
For the pie

Mixing bowl • Cutting board
Rolling pin • Skewer • Pastry brush
Small star-shaped cutter • Pie plate
Bowl • Potato peeler • Large spoon
Sharp knife

For the custard

Saucepan
Wooden spoon • Bowl

For the pastry

2 cups all-purpose flour

A pinch of salt

¼ cup vegetable shortening or lard

Small amount of water

2 tablespoons sugar

4 tablespoons butter

For the filling

1 teaspoon ground cinnamon

2 lbs (about 6) cooking apples

3 tablespoons brown sugar

1 tablespoon cornstarch

For the custard

2 tablespoons superfine sugar

4 egg yolks

2²/₃ cups milk

2 tablespoons cornstarch

2 drops vanilla extract

Making the pie

Set the oven to 400°F.
Rub the flour, butter, and
shortening together in the
mixing bowl.

2 When the mixture is like fine
bread crumbs, add the sugar,
then add about 3 tablespoons
water and mix it in well.

3 Gently *knead* the mixture
into a ball of *dough*. If the
dough seems too crumbly, add a
little more water.

Peel the apples and cut them
into quarters. Cut out the
cores and seeds, then cut each
apple quarter in half.

5 Put the sliced apples in a
bowl. Add the brown sugar,
cornstarch, and cinnamon and
mix everything together.

6 Sprinkle flour on the table and
roll out three-quarters of the
pastry into a circle 1/4 inch thick
and bigger than the pie plate.

7 Lay the pie plate on top of
the pastry and cut around it.
Then cut a strip of pastry to go
around the edge of the plate.

8 Press the pastry strip around
the edge and brush it with
water. Put the apples in the pie
plate and lay the pastry on top.

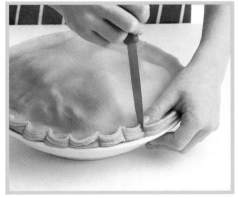

9 Press the edges of the pastry
together and trim them.
Then make a pattern around
them with a knife, as shown.

DECORATING THE PIE

1 *Roll out* the pastry you have left. Cut two-thirds of it into narrow strips and cut small stars out of the rest with a cutter.

2 Brush the pastry with water. Make a cross with two long strips and add stripes with the rest. Prick air holes with the skewer.

3 Lay stars on the rest of the pastry, then sprinkle it with sugar. *Bake* the pie for 45 minutes, until golden brown.

Other decorations

We have used stars and stripes to make an all–American apple pie, but you can decorate a pie with any shapes you like. Choose a theme, or just use the cutters you have at home.

Hot from the oven

Serve the apple pie hot, along wit a pitcher of homemade custard to pour on top. Or try it with thick whipped cream.

LOVING HEARTS

LEAFY APPLES

GRACEFUL FLOWER

Making the custard

1 Heat the milk in a saucepan over medium heat until it starts to look frothy on top. Take the pan off the heat.

2 Mix the egg yolks, sugar, vanilla extract, and cornstarch together in a bowl. Then stir in the hot milk, a little at a time.

3 Pour the mixture back into the saucepan and cook it over low heat. Stir it until it has thickened to a creamy sauce.

CUSTARD

APPLE PIE

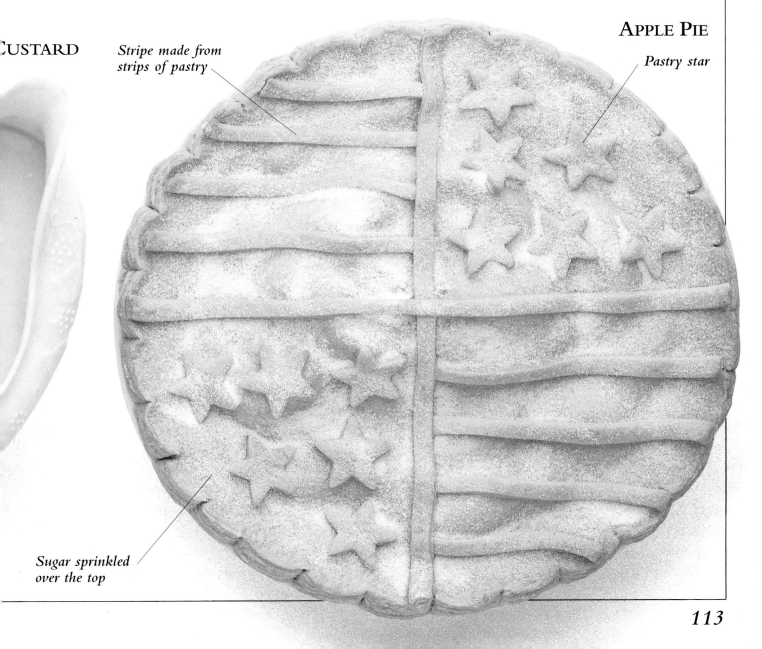

Stripe made from strips of pastry

Pastry star

Sugar sprinkled over the top

CREPES

Make these foolproof crêpes and fill them with whatever you like. With practice you should get 12 crêpes out of the amounts given here. Stack the crêpes on a warm plate as you make them and fill them when ready to eat.

You will need (for 12 servings)

A pinch of salt

2 eggs

1 cup all-purpose flour

4 tablespoons melted butter

²/₃ cup milk and ²/₃ cup water mixed together

What to do

1 Put the flour and salt in a bowl. Add the eggs and some of the milk and water, and *whisk* in the flour, a little at a time.

2 Then gradually pour the remaining milk and water into the mixture, whisking it until the ingredients are well mixed in.

3 Add half the melted butter to the mixture and whisk it again. This smooth, creamy mixture is called the *batter*.

4 Brush the skillet pan with a little melted butter and heat until it sizzles. Then pour in two tablespoonfuls of batter.

5 Quickly tilt the pan from side to side until a thin layer of batter spreads across the bottom of the skillet.

6 Cook the crêpe for about a minute, then flip it over, cook it for 10 more seconds and slide it onto a warm plate.

Hot crêpes

When you are ready to eat, spread the crêpes with filling and roll or fold them in any of the ways shown here.

HAM PACKAGES

FANS

Try spreading the crêpes with honey and folding them into triangles.

Or sprinkle your crêpes with lemon juice and sugar and simply roll them up.

These crêpes were spread with jam and folded into quarters.

LEMON ROLLS

115

PICNIC TIME

Why not put together a picnic using recipes from the book? Wrap things in aluminum foil, arrange homemade bread rolls in baskets, and put salad in containers.

FILLED ROLLS
(pages 20–21)

GREEK SALAD
(pages 56–57)

TARTS
(pages 36–39)

**FRESH
BREAD ROLL**
(pages 84–87)

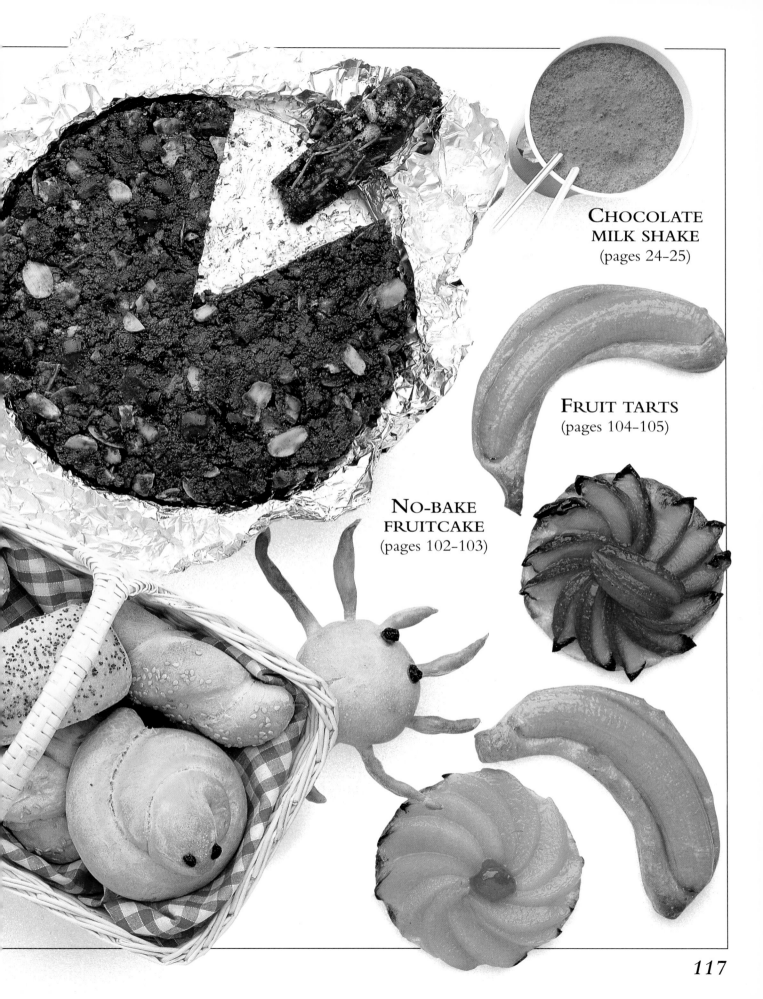

CHOCOLATE MILK SHAKE
(pages 24–25)

FRUIT TARTS
(pages 104–105)

NO-BAKE FRUITCAKE
(pages 102–103)

117

PARTY TIME

Choose the most colorful recipes from the book for your party. Start with savory snacks, then move on to sweet things, and finish with a special birthday cake.

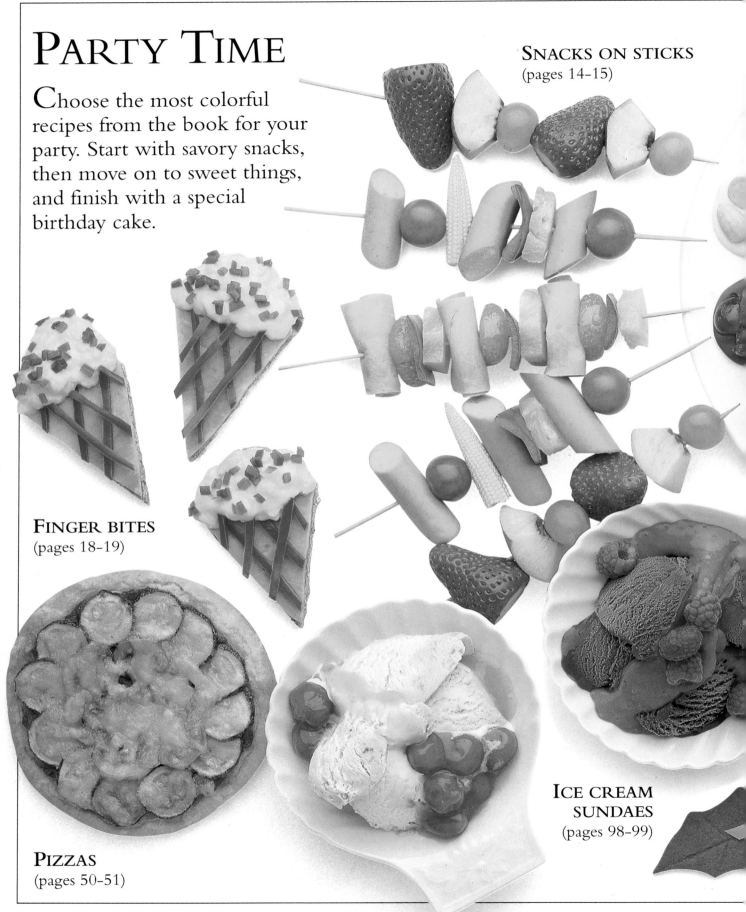

SNACKS ON STICKS
(pages 14–15)

FINGER BITES
(pages 18–19)

ICE CREAM SUNDAES
(pages 98–99)

PIZZAS
(pages 50–51)

MILK SHAKE
(pages 24-25)

ICED
SPONGE
CAKE
(pages 92-95)

ICED CUPCAKES
(pages 88-91)

GINGERBREAD FOLK (pages 78-81)

MENU PLANNER

Here are some ideas for meals you can put together from recipes in this book. When you are planning a meal, try to choose things with contrasting flavors, colors, and textures. Choose the main course first, then plan the rest of the meal around it.

A PIZZA FEAST

Pizzas
(pages 50-51)

Fruit kabobs *(pages 14-15)*

A SUMMERY MEAL

Greek salad *(pages 56-57)*

Fresh bread rolls *(pages 84-87)*

Crêpes *(pages 114-115)*

ITALIAN-STYLE LUNCH

Creamy spaghetti *(pages 42-43)*

Green salad *(pages 56-57)*

Ice cream sundaes *(pages 98-99)*

VEGETARIAN MEAL

Vegetables and rice *(pages 46-47)*

Fruit tarts *(pages 104-105)*

WINTER WARMER

Beef stew *(pages 72-73)*

Boiled potatoes and broccoli
(pages 54-55)

Apple pie and custard
(pages 110-113)

EXOTIC LUNCH

Spicy chicken *(pages 70-71)*
Boiled rice *(page 46)*

Fruit baskets *(pages 108-109)*

FAST FOOD

Hamburgers *(pages 66-67)*

Milk shakes *(pages 24-25)*

PICTURE GLOSSARY

This is a picture guide to some of the special terms that cooks use most often. Here you can find out what each term means and learn, step-by-step, how to master the most useful basic cooking skills.

Slicing

To slice vegetables, hold them firmly on a chopping board and slice downward. Hold the knife against your knuckles, as shown, so you do not cut your fingers.

Chopping herbs

To chop fresh herbs such as parsley, bunch the stalks together and hold them down on the board while you slice the leaves finely.

Shredding lettuce

Hold the lettuce down on a board and cut across it in very fine slices. This will give you thin ribbons of lettuce.

Dicing

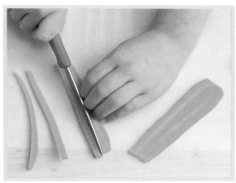

1 Dicing means to cut into small cubes. To dice a vegetable, cut it in half length-wise, then cut it into thin strips.

2 Now hold the strips together and slice through them to make small cubes.

Chopping an onion

1 Peel the onion, leaving the root on to hold the onion together.

2 Cut the onion in half and lay one half, cut side down, on the chopping board. Then use a sharp knife to make downward cuts in the onion.

3 Turn the onion and make cuts at right angles across the first cuts, to chop the onion.

Preparing fresh ginger root

1 Ginger root has a woody skin. Use a sharp knife to cut the skin off the piece of root.

2 Slice the ginger root finely. Cut the slices into thin strips, then slice through them to make small cubes.

Peeling and crushing garlic

1 Gently pull the garlic cloves away from the bulb of garlic with your fingers.

2 Peel the skin away from the clove of garlic, then put the garlic in a garlic press and close the handle to press the garlic through the holes.

Coring an apple

1 Wash the apple, then push the corer into the apple around the core, right down to the base.

2 Pull the corer out again, to remove a cylinder of apple containing the core and seeds.

Grating cheese

Hold the grater down firmly on a chopping board or plate and rub the cheese downward against the grater, keeping your fingers well away from it.

Pitting fruit

1 Cut the fruit in half with a sharp knife, following the crease down the side of it.

2 Then take the fruit in both hands and twist each half, to loosen it from the pit.

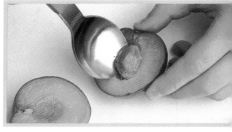

3 Scoop the pit out of the fruit with a spoon.

Dough

This is the term for a thick mixture made mainly of flour before it has been cooked. It can be cake, bread, cookie, or pastry dough.

Batter

A flour-based mixture that is runny enough to pour, such as crêpe batter.

Sifting

To sift flour or confectioners' sugar, shake it through a sieve. This gets rid of lumps and makes it light and airy.

Creaming

1 To cream butter and sugar together, cut up the butter and rub it into the sugar in a bowl using a wooden spoon.

2 Then beat the butter and sugar together as hard as you can with the wooden spoon.

3 The mixture is ready when it is pale and creamy and drops off the spoon easily.

Rubbing in

To do this, rub butter or margarine and flour together with your fingertips until the mixture looks like fine breadcrumbs.

Folding in

This is a gentle way of mixing. Using a large spoon or rubber spatula, "cut" into the mixture, then turn and lift to mix.

Kneading

To knead dough, fold it and punch it down, then turn it around and keep doing the same thing until the dough is smooth and stretchy.

123

Beating

To beat something, stir it hard. Beat eggs with a fork or whisk until the yolks and whites are mixed together.

Separating an egg

1 Crack the egg near the middle by tapping it gently against a bowl.

2 Then break the egg open with your thumbs and tip the yolk from one half of the shell to the other, so that the white slips into the bowl below. Put the yolk in a separate bowl.

Whisking

1 To whisk egg whites, beat them quickly and lightly with a whisk.

2 Continue whisking until the whites are firm and stand up in peaks.

Scoring bread

To score bread, slash the top of the dough with a sharp knife, cutting about 1/2 inch deep to make lines.

Rolling out pastry

1 Sprinkle the table and rolling pin with flour and roll the ball of dough out away from you

2 Then lift the dough, turn it and roll it again, sprinkling with more flour if needed. Keep doing this until the dough forms the shape you want.

Glazing

Glazing means to coat food with something to make it look glossy. This tart is being brushed with jam.

Seasoning

When you season food, you add salt, pepper, spices, or herbs to it. This gives it extra flavor.

Marinating

To marinate meat, fish, or vegetables, you soak them in a special sauce before cooking them. This adds flavor and makes the food more tender.

Blending

Blending means mixing ingredients together in a blender or food processor. Make sure the lid of the blender is firmly closed.

Grilling

To grill food, you cook it quickly at a high temperature under a grill or broiler.

Simmering

Simmering means cooking liquid over a low heat so that it is bubbling gently, but not boiling.

Boiling

Boiling means cooking in water that is boiling (bubbling rapidly).

Frying

To fry food, cook it in hot fat or oil until it is brown and crisp.

Stir-frying

To stir-fry vegetables or meat, put them in a wok or frying pan with a small amount of oil or fat, and cook quickly over a very high heat, stirring all the time.

Baking

To bake is to cook in an oven.

Lining a cake pan

1 Lay the cake pan face down on a sheet of waxed paper and draw around it. Then cut out the circle of paper.

2 Brush the inside of the cake pan with melted butter.

3 Then lay the circle of waxed paper inside the pan and brush it with more melted butter.

Making an icing bag

1 Cut out a piece of waxed paper 10 inches square and fold it in half diagonally.

2 Fold one corner of the folded triangle into the middle point to make a cone.

3 Fold the other corner of the triangle around it so that the three points meet.

4 Then tuck the points inside the cone to hold it firmly in place. Snip the tip off the cone.

Greasing a pan or dish

To grease a baking pan or ovenproof dish, rub it with butter, oil, or margarine. This stops food from sticking to it.

Piping icing

Fill the icing bag with icing. Fold the top of the bag down over the icing and press gently to squeeze out a thin ribbon of icing through the tip of the cone.

Dorling Kindersley would like to than
Christopher Gillingwater, Robin Hunter, an
Rachael Foster for additional design help;
Polly Goodman for additional editorial help;
Emma Patmore for cooking assistance;
and Jonathan Buckley, Polly Arber, Serina
Palmer, Selena Singh, and Phoebe Thoms
for modeling.